A HISTORY OF DEATH IN

17TH CENTURY ENGLAND

A HISTORY OF DEATH IN
17TH
CENTURY
ENGLAND

BEN NORMAN

PEN & SWORD
HISTORY

AN IMPRINT OF PEN & SWORD BOOKS LTD
YORKSHIRE - PHILADELPHIA

First published in Great Britain in 2020 by
PEN AND SWORD HISTORY
An imprint of
Pen & Sword Books Ltd
Yorkshire - Philadelphia

ISBN 978 1 52675 526 1

Typeset in Times New Roman 11.5/14 by
SJmagic DESIGN SERVICES, India.
Printed and bound in the UK by CPI Books Ltd.

Pen & Sword Books Ltd incorporates the Imprints of Pen & Sword Books
Archaeology, Atlas, Aviation, Battleground, Discovery, Family History, History,
Maritime, Military, Naval, Politics, Railways, Select, Transport, True Crime,
Fiction, Frontline Books, Leo Cooper, Praetorian Press, Seaforth Publishing,
Wharncliffe and White Owl.

For a complete list of Pen & Sword titles please contact
PEN & SWORD BOOKS LIMITED
47 Church Street, Barnsley, South Yorkshire, S70 2AS, England
E-mail: enquiries@pen-and-sword.co.uk
Website: www.pen-and-sword.co.uk

Or
PEN AND SWORD BOOKS
1950 Lawrence Rd, Havertown, PA 19083, USA
E-mail: Uspen-and-sword@casematepublishers.com
Website: www.penandswordbooks.com

Contents

Abbreviations

PCCRP   Prerogative Court of Canterbury and Related Probate Jurisdictions

Author's Note

Quotations from primary source material have retained their original spelling and grammar where applicable. To the best of the author's knowledge and ability dates within this book are in line with the Julian calendar, which was the calendar in use in seventeenth-century England and at the time was roughly 10 days behind the present-day Gregorian calendar. The Gregorian calendar was adopted in England in 1752. All years (again to the best of the author's knowledge and ability) are presented as beginning on 1 January, although in the 1600s it was common to celebrate the New Year on 25 March.

Picture Acknowledgements

In the book

Picture Acknowledgements

23. Public Domain, from the British Library's collections, 2013
24. Wellcome Collection. CC BY
25. Wellcome Collection. CC BY
26. Author's private collection
27. Author's private collection
28. Author's private collection
29. Author's private collection
30. Author's private collection
31. Author's private collection
32. Author's private collection
33. Author's private collection
34. Jacob Truedson Demitz for Ristesson History [Public domain]
35. The Portable Antiquities Scheme/The Trustees of the British Museum [CC BY-SA 2.0 (https://creativecommons.org/licenses/by-sa/2.0)]

On the cover

1. (Townspeople fleeing to the countryside to escape the plague in England, 1630. Hand-coloured woodcut.) North Wind Picture Archives / Alamy Stock Photo
2. (The beheading of Charles I outside the Banqueting Hall of Whitehall in 1649. Engraving with etching.) Wellcome Collection. CC BY
3. (Surgeons performing an operation on a woman's breast in the seventeenth century.) Wellcome Collection. CC BY

Chapter headers

1. (Skull on a book) Public Domain, from the British Library's collections, 2013

ix

Acknowledgements and Dedications

I wish to thank Pen and Sword Books for giving me the incentive to follow through with this project and agreeing to publish the book, particularly as I am a first-time author. My particular thanks go to Aileen at P&S for answering the many questions I had throughout the process. More generally I would like to thank my family and friends (you know who you are) for their support and encouragement, and for assuring me that the topic sounded interesting. The proof of the pudding is in the reading.

Bearing in mind that this book is as much about life as it is death, I am keen to dedicate it to two individuals: Joy Bradford, who sadly departed this world three years ago now, and baby Alba-Rose, who as I type these words is not three weeks old and has her whole life ahead of her.

Ben Norman, August 2019

1. Death as king, by an unknown engraver.

Introduction

On entering his fiftieth year in 1673, Sir Edward Harley of Herefordshire noted:

'O Lord! in thy hand is the breath of all mankind, and it is only God who holdeth our soul in life. But in most special manner I ought to praise my God, who preserved me from abortion at Burton-under-the-Hill. In this place, this day gave the light of life to poor clay, and for forty-nine years thou hast granted me life and favour, and thy visitation hath preserved my spirit. Lord, thou hast granted me life in the deliverances of life: when a child, from the chin-cough, measles, small-pox twice, and danger of drowning in the moat; when a man, from many perils in the wars, particularly when my horse was shot, when my arm was hurt, when a muskett-bullett, levelled at my heart, was bent flat against my armour, not reckoned of such proof, without any harm to myself. [...] I have often been preserved in journeys and voyages from thieves; from waters, specially in a dangerous passage once at Newnham. Many times I crossed the sea between England and Flanders, allways safely [...] I was delivered from the malitious accusation of the army, 1647, and my God made my speech in my defence in Parliament acceptable. That year I was preserved from the plague, of which my servant died, and at the same time recovered from a dangerous pestilential fever.'[1]

Harley recognised that he was lucky to be alive. He was of the opinion that many different things could have killed him in the long years between his birth and the present day. As an infant he had been in danger of succumbing to a succession of childhood diseases, including 'chincough' (better known today as whooping cough), measles, and smallpox, the latter of which he had managed to catch twice. As a man he was no safer. Armed conflict brought its own risks, some too horrific to contemplate, and had endangered his life on several occasions. During the English Civil War, Harley was mercifully spared from a shot to the heart by a musket bullet only because it bounced off his armour. He acknowledged that it was something of a miracle that he had not been set upon and killed by thieves while on the road, as many others had been, or that he had survived numerous sea crossings when so many sailors had drowned. The Member of Parliament found it incredible that he had successfully avoided the plague, too, even though it had killed thousands of defenceless victims, including his own servant.

Edward Harley had dodged the bullet several times, sometimes literally, in the first 49 years of his earthly existence. His reflections reveal that there were countless ways in which individuals could, and did, die in seventeenth-century England. The struggle for life started from the moment a baby was born. Although seeing some improvement in the early years of the century, infant mortality rates were worse than they had been for over 100 years by 1700. In 1642 the preacher John Toy lamented the downward trend, begging the question, 'How many come only to suck a Bib, or shake a Ratle, and returne again to earth?'. For adults and children alike, the dangers posed from infectious diseases were ever-present. Plague might finish you during its frequent outbreaks up to the 1660s, as it finished Harley's poor servant in 1647. If plague passed you by, you might find yourself dying as a result of smallpox instead, a complaint that would not fully disappear from the country, as hard as it is to believe, until three centuries later in 1978. A whole host of other sicknesses could claim the life of an individual in the 1600s. A simple fever might prove fatal, and often was in children. The more overtly dangerous conditions of tuberculosis, the 'bloody flux', and dropsy, greatly feared by the vicar Ralph Josselin in the 1680s, were killers too.

If one did not die a natural death, one might easily expire unnaturally. War laid waste to the land in the 1640s and killed thousands of men, women, and children in unspeakable ways. Some died bleeding out in fields, while others were torn apart – limb from limb – by the deluge of ammunition that pelted besieged cities up and down the country. Edward Harley had been fortunate indeed when a bullet was parried by his armour in the midst of an unnamed attack, but it was an ugly reality that innumerable soldiers were not shown the same mercy. Following the Battle of Marston Moor in 1644 the Parliamentarian, Lionel Watson gave an account of the final moments of the fighting. By 9.00pm Parliament's forces had emptied the battlefield of the opposing Royalist army, giving chase to them as they fled in the direction of York. The king's men were cut down 'so that their dead bodies lay three miles in length'.

The English Civil War was disastrous in terms of its ultimate death toll. It ought to have dissuaded the nation from ever associating itself with unnecessary bloodshed again. The criminal justice system, however, only added to the large numbers of unnatural deaths occurring in England in the seventeenth century. Felonious hangings were a common sight before and after the civil war. They were attended by hundreds of people if the crime committed had been particularly offensive, or the criminal being executed was well-known. Hanging, drawing, and quartering was also used to a lesser extent, as were beheadings in exceptional cases. The public were not shielded from such events, but were encouraged to attend and revel in the violence on display. Not all spectators enjoyed what they saw. As the murderer Nathaniel Butler rode in a coach on his way to be hanged in Cheapside in 1657, the crowds watching 'prayed for his soul, and shewed compassion otherwise to him', as opposed to baying for blood.

Death at the opportunistic hands of a murderer constituted another way in which some met their end in seventeenth-century England. Nathaniel Butler's homicidal actions are a case in point. In the August before his execution, while apprenticed as a clothier to a Mr Goodday in Carter Lane, London, Butler leapt at the opportunity to steal several bags of money in a shop on nearby Milk Street. To ensure his crime was successful he came to the conclusion that it would be prudent to first kill the companion with whom he often shared a bed above the shop in question. On the night of the robbery the events were thus:

'At night they lay again together, the bloody design running still in the mind of Butler: he intending about the dead of the night…to destroy the Young man by cutting his throat: Accordingly he took his knife in his hand, but his heart would not suffer him to do it; then he laid down the knife again, yea, he took up and laid down his knife several times…before he acted his cruelty: But in the morning very early he did indeed fall very violently and inhumanely on the Youth, who lay harmlesly asleep upon the bed. The first wound not being mortal, awaked him, whereupon he strugled and made a noise…which was heard into another room of the same house. Then Butler chopt his fist into the mouth of the Young man, and so they two lay striving and tumbling very near half an hour, before the fatal blow was given.'[2]

Having committed the murder, he then:

'went down, taking away out of the shop a sum of money in two bags, being about One hundred and ten pounds: And so with his double guilt of Robbery and Murder, leaving his bloody Shirt behind him, and a Lock of his own hair in the hand of the dead Young-man…he went to his Masters house in Carter-lane, where he privately laid the Money in a new Trunk that he bought with part of the money.'[3]

Murder was a popular topic in contemporary accounts of the period, including diaries. In July 1634 William Whiteway of Dorchester recorded with apparent fascination that a man had been taken to Poole and 'hanged there in chaines for killing and cutting in pieces a maide to whome he was a suter'.

With all this in mind, we can deduce that death was a ubiquitous part of life in seventeenth-century England. It infiltrated families, invaded the public sphere, and generally shaded lives in a way that is quite unthinkable in the twenty-first century. Any history of England at this time would be sorely lacking without a concerted look at such a fundamental topic. This book will chart the history of death in seventeenth-century England using a chronological approach, beginning with how people died and finishing with how they were remembered once they had been laid to rest, and touching on every formality and customary occurrence in between. A major theme explored is the sweeping changes that were affecting the rituals surrounding death, burial, and remembrance in the seventeenth century. Long-established medieval customs were giving way to new practices and techniques inspired by the country's conversion to Protestantism the previous century. Modes of remembrance in particular were altered to suit the attitudes of a country that was beginning to view death in a much more practical and final sense, as a veil through which it was impossible to reach.

Chapter 1

The Natural Death

Natural death could strike at an early age in seventeenth-century England. It was not uncommon for a baby to die soon after leaving its mother's womb. If the child was fortunate enough to survive for more than a few days, there was still a good chance that it would be dead before it had reached its milestone first birthday. Mortality rates for infants below the age of one were resolutely grim throughout the century, with roughly 165 out of every 1,000 babies born expected to die before they had turned a year old in the first 25 years after 1600. The next quarter-century saw this figure drop slightly, to 153 out of every 1,000 infants, but in the latter 50 years of the 1600s the statistics climbed sharply again. From 1675 until the turn of the eighteenth century, close to one in five births resulted in the death of the child before the celebration of its first birthday.

The death of a newborn baby in seventeenth-century England could be quick and distressing. The country squire Nicholas Assheton recorded in February 1618 that his wife had undergone a labour so ferocious that the infant was dead only half an hour after being delivered. Alice Thornton, an autobiographer residing in North Yorkshire, complained before the imminent birth of her daughter in 1652 that the unborn child, 'was greatly forced with violent motions perpetually, till it grew soe weake that it had left stirring'. Her daughter was delivered and pronounced dead after a mere 30 minutes of life, not living long enough even to be baptised, although a minister was sent for in case she survived.

Those infants that survived the initial birth, but which were nonetheless destined to die young, arguably faced a more traumatic end.

Alice Thornton vividly recorded the premature deaths of several of her children, disclosing to posterity the awful experience through which many parents were forced to live. Her son, William Thornton, died less than a fortnight after being born in 1660. After a 'hard' and 'hazardous' labour, her initial reaction was that she had been blessed with a 'happie child'. The Friday following the birth, however, things changed rapidly. Having had William dressed in the morning, she noticed that he had become unsettled and irritated. After three hours of sleep, the situation had taken another undesirable turn, with the child breaking out in 'red round spotts' the size of halfpennies and 'all whealed white over'. Alice tried to comfort her ailing child, holding him in her arms as he slept, and remarking that every so often he would lift his eyes to the ceiling, as if he 'saw angells in heaven'. Perhaps he had. That night young Willy Thornton's sickness took hold completely and fatally. On Saturday morning the baby died, leaving Alice bereft that he had been taken from her so soon. Alice's husband took the news equally as badly, lamenting that he had lost a son and heir.

Ralph Josselin, vicar of Earls Colne in Essex from 1640, suffered a similar blow in February 1648. His wife gave birth to a son on 11 February, which was in his view the 'easiest and speediest labour that ever shee had'. By the seventeenth day of that month, however, the child was severely ill and 'full of phlegme', causing a physician to be promptly sent for who attempted to revive baby Ralph with a remedy of syrup of roses. At this point Jane Josselin, the child's mother, was convinced that her son would die. Ralph Senior similarly expected the infant to be dead by the following morning. The child survived the night to the great relief of his parents, but the warning signs were there for all to see, and Ralph swiftly set about organising for his son to be baptised and formally admitted into the Christian Church. The tiny infant was accordingly washed and sanctified the following day. The child's condition had not improved by 19 February, by which time Ralph had resigned himself to the fact that his sick offspring would not be recovering. Drawing strength from his religious convictions, so imperative to the life of a seventeenth-century English citizen, he soothed himself and his wife by maintaining that little Ralph would soon be in 'the land of rest, where there is no sicknes nor childhood but all perfection'. That night the baby cried less, but Ralph noted that it kept up a distressingly frothy mouth; the next morning, the despairing father witnessed 'some redd mattery stuffe' coming out in place of the foam. The end was near. On 21 February, a mere 10 days after his birth, with such promise of life ahead of him, baby Ralph departed the world without uttering a sound. Ralph Senior turned back to religion to ease his bereavement, commenting in his diary that God had been merciful in giving him and his wife time to prepare for the child's passing.

Reaching a first birthday did not by any means signal that the danger of dying a premature death was over, as Ralph Josselin would have been all too aware. Seventeenth-century England witnessed many cases of children dying before their tenth birthday, including Ralph's daughter Mary. His diary entries suggest that Mary had been sick for some time before her condition suddenly worsened. He relayed that on 22 May 1650, just two years after the death of his son, his eight-year-old daughter was dangerously ill with worms. Ralph hurriedly ventured down to Colne Priory to fetch some medicine back for his sick child, feeling hopeful that she would make a full recovery from the ailment with the assistance of an earthly remedy. He came home to find that she had passed a stool containing three 'great dead wormes', a good sign, and the next day he remarked that she had successfully 'voyded' six more. In the morning she slept peacefully, another good sign, but by nightfall the terminal gravity of her sickness was evident. Ralph was woken by his wife in the middle of the night, sobbing that Mary was dying. The following morning all hopes of saving this young girl's life were extinguished, and as he had done with his baby son, Ralph offered his daughter up into the reassuring arms of the Lord. She died on 27 May, to the utter lamentation of her father:

> 'This day a quarter past two in ye afternoone my Mary fell asleepe in the Lord […] shee was 8 yeares and 45 dayes old when shee dyed; my soule had aboundant cause to blesse God for her, who was our first fruites […] it was a pretious child, a bundle of myrrhe, a bundle of sweetnes; shee was a child of ten thousand, full of wisedome, womanlike gravity, knowledge […] tender hearted & loving […] it was to us as a boxe of sweet ointment; which now its broken smells more deliciously then it did before.'[1]

The extent to which a parent grieved for their deceased child depended on how old the child was at the time of his or her death. The general rule of thumb stipulated that the younger a child was when it perished, the less inclined the parents would be to express an outpouring of genuine sorrow for the loss. Part of the reason for this trend probably stemmed from the underdevelopment of the bond of affection between a newborn baby and its parents, as well as from the tendency for early modern individuals to view tiny infants as not-quite-developed people. Nicholas Assheton may have lost a child merely half an hour after its coming into the world in 1618, but that did not stop him from embarking on a carefree hunt in the snow the following day. John Evelyn, the famous writer, diarist, and resident of London, was somewhat reserved when recounting the death of his son John, who died of 'convulsion-fits' in January 1654 at the age of just three months. The passing of his son Richard in 1658, who had reached the age of five when he succumbed to an ague and thus was much older than his younger brother had been, was much harder for the writer to bear. Describing how Richard had suffered 'six fits of a quartan ague', Evelyn continued that, 'it pleased God to visit him…to our inexpressible grief and affliction'. The enormous pain of losing his five-year-old boy was laid bare in the passionate admiration he expressed for his deceased son and his many extraordinary talents, especially for one so young. Evelyn wrote feverishly in his diary about the number of languages the boy could read, the unequalled ability he possessed for conjugating foreign verbs and memorising Latin and French vocabulary, and the 'astonishing' piety Richard had demonstrated as a Christian, particularly in his understanding of the historical parts of the Bible. The writer remarked that, 'he was all life, all prettiness, far from morose, sullen, or childish in any thing he said or did'. The modern reader would be forgiven for thinking that he was describing a literate teenager of 15, not a little boy of five. He would clearly be sorely missed.

The trauma of losing a child could still affect a parent years later. Mary Rich, Countess of Warwick, took to marking the day of her son's death annually as a way in which to channel her continued grief. In 1667 she wrote:

'I kept a private fast, being the day three years upon which my son died. As soon as up, I retired into the garden to meditate; had there large meditations upon the sickness and death of my only child, upon all his sick-bed expressions, and the manner how God was pleased to awaken him, with which thoughts my heart was much affected.'[2]

Lady Warwick was fortunate to be alive herself. Childbirth risked the life of the mother as well as endangering the prospective life of the baby. It is estimated that throughout the whole of the seventeenth century a mother had a one per cent chance of dying during her pregnancy or in labour, making it a considerably riskier business than childbearing in the twenty-first century. Oliver Heywood, a nonconformist minister living in the north of England, reported in 1684 that he had heard of two women dying in childbirth in a single day in Bradford, with another woman dying the day after in the same tragic fashion. Very soon after these deaths, Heywood stated that his wife had been called to the bedside of yet another expectant mother who had fallen ill during the trials and tribulations of early modern labour. In this case the mother survived; the child did not. Although the wealthier sort might have more ready access to physicians and other professionals while inhabiting the childbed, this did not necessarily mean that the risk of maternal death was any less present for them. The daughter-in-law of Robert Sidney, Earl of Leicester, was said to have 'delivered of a daughter very well' in Charing Cross in 1652, but the next day she was gripped by a violent fever that caused her to 'lose her senses'. The physicians could do nothing for her, and so she died.

Although it was quite acceptable for an individual to count themselves lucky in the event that they survived the hazards of childhood in seventeenth-century England, they were by no means left invincible as an adolescent or adult. Life expectancy was low even for grown men and women. An adult might reach the age of 60 and consider it a fortunate stroke of luck, but most people living in the 1600s could expect a lifespan of somewhere between 30 and 40 years. To the modern observer living in England in the twenty-first century, this is a startlingly young age, tantamount to dying in the prime of life. For those residing in the country four centuries ago, this would have been nothing more or less than the accepted norm. Early onsets of disease were a considerable killer, the prevalence of which has led some to believe that it is likely that most people felt ill most of the time in the seventeenth century.

While by no means the biggest killer disease of the period, bubonic plague is often remembered as the worst. Its horrible symptoms, coupled with the cruel way in which it snatched away whole families and decimated entire towns, has meant that even today the sickness holds a fearsome reputation in the popular imagination. England suffered a deadly outbreak of plague in the middle of the fourteenth century. Known to posterity as the Black Death, it has been reasonably suggested that during this visitation up to a third or even half of the population was totally wiped out by the disease. By the beginning of the seventeenth century plague had become much less devastating in England, but frightening and considerable outbreaks were still known to occur until the mid-1660s. Significant visitations of bubonic plague occurred in the country in 1603, 1625, 1636, and 1665, mainly affecting London and those unlucky towns that straddled major trade routes out of the capital. The disease's symptoms were ugly. After receiving the fateful fleabite, sufferers were struck down with a high temperature that led to excruciating headaches, vomiting, agitation, and confusion. At the same time, black carbuncles burst out of the skin wherever the victim had been bitten, and the lymph nodes in any of the groin, armpit, or neck began to swell and fester, giving the infected individual a swollen, unsightly appearance. A contemporary observer of the plague marvelled at the number of different symptoms that sufferers could display during an outbreak, commenting that one week 'the general distempers' might be 'botches and boils', the next 'clear-skinned as may be'. He continued:

> 'One week, full of spots and tokens; and perhaps the succeeding, none at all. Now taken with a vomiting and looseness, and within two or three days almost a general raging madness. One while patients used to linger four or five days, at other times not forty-eight hours; and at this very time we find it more quick than ever it was. Many are sick, and few escape. Where it has had its fling, there it decreases; where it has not been long, there it increases.'[3]

The plague brought with it upon every major visitation in seventeenth-century England varying levels of fear, frenzy, and disarray. The lawyer and merchant Walter Yonge, writing from the safety of Devon in 1603, commented with apparent terror that London had undergone that year 'the greatest pestilence that ever was heard of or known by any man living', reporting anxiously that at its height 3,000 people were dying every week. The plague travelled north in 1604 to York, causing further disorder and resulting in the deaths of over 3,500 of its helpless citizens, a third of the city's population. In an attempt to quell the spread of infection York Minster was shut up, the city's markets were suspended, and the diseased were rounded up and taken to plague lodges or booths at various designated locations on the outskirts of the town, where fate would decide whether they lived or died. London was faced with two more lethal onslaughts of black carbuncles and unsightly swellings in 1625 and 1630. The 1630 visitation sped northwards to East Anglia, breaking out in the spring at Cambridge and Norwich and causing wealthy town dwellers to flee in panic into the surrounding countryside. In May the Reverend John Rous wrote in his diary that three houses had been shut up in Norwich, a measure resulting from official instructions stipulating that buildings housing sick residents should be quarantined at all costs in order to stem the spread of infection. But for many the plague was simply unstoppable. During the summer of 1630 Rous reported that the pestilence was still very 'sore' in Cambridge, to such an extent that the Stourbridge fair held annually in the town had been cancelled.

The powerful influence of religion in seventeenth-century England caused many to view the coming of plague as a divine punishment from God for the sins of mankind. Reflecting on the outbreak that struck Newcastle in 1636, the religious merchant John Fenwick stated gravely that God had spoken to the town's citizens by mortally infecting 5,500 people and making the streets grow 'greene with grasse'. The Reverend Edward Burghall, writing earlier in 1631 following a visitation of the plague in Lancashire, agreed wholeheartedly with this celestial explanation. He believed that Cheshire had been protected from the sickness only because public fasts had 'turned away' God's hand, leaving other areas, such as Preston, to be depopulated and turned rotten. If this was the case, then the epidemic of 1665 was by far God's harshest biological punishment of the century. Approximately 100,000 people would die in the catastrophic event that has become known as the Great Plague of London, although in actual fact it affected many areas outside of the capital too. None would be exempt from God's arrow, barring those who could afford to leave the city quickly. Citizens living in squalor in London's slums were invariably doomed to an uncertain, and often unpleasant, fate. Plenty would be reduced to a death in the gutter. Officials and professionals with religious and civil obligations, such as vicars and searchers (the latter consisting of women hired to seek out corpses and determine the cause of death), were likewise vulnerable to infection. Hysteria and paranoia would reach fever pitch as many obsessed over the incessant weekly recordings of the number of plague deaths in the capital printed in the Bills of Mortality, which seemed to stack higher with every new edition. The Great Plague was a blight on the English people like no other epidemic in the seventeenth century had been before it, but it would also bring a resounding end to the sporadic outbreaks of major plague in the country.

The first isolated cases of plague were reported in London in late 1664. By the spring of 1665 the disease had reared its fearsome head again, but this time it was more worrying, for the hot summer months were a period in which plague was known to thrive. Samuel Pepys, the famous London diarist, noted nervously on 30 April that there were 'great fears of the sicknesse here in the City, it being said that two or three houses are already shut up'. A month later he recorded that the plague was 'growing upon us in this towne'. By June, it was clear that London was sliding into a serious epidemic. On the twenty-ninth Pepys noticed 'against his will' that two or three houses were shut up in Drury Lane, with red crosses painted on the doors of each and the words 'Lord have mercy upon us' written alongside them. News began to reach the provinces that the plague – that *dreaded* disease – was on course to overrun the capital, provoking frantic responses from concerned family members. Sir Ralph Verney's Aunt Isham urged her nephew to wear a quill filled with quicksilver, sealed with hard wax, and sewn up in a 'silke thinge' around his neck for protection against the disease while he was in town. July saw the mass exodus of 1,800 families from London as the plague began to take hold in earnest, by which time King Charles II and his courtiers had already fled to Hampton Court. The poor could do nothing but stay and pray. Ralph Josselin, watching events unfold agitatedly from Earls Colne, wrote on 9 July that, 'the plague feares the Londoners; they flie before it and the country feares all trade with London'. On 28 July he reported again that the 'plague grows hott; persons fall down in London streets, 1843 of plague'. Five days later, he partook in the first monthly public fast for the capital, which his parish hoped would convince God to stop the disease in its tracks.

The Bills of Mortality announced the deaths of 2,817 from plague in London in August 1665. It was now the height of summer, the worst time of year in which to attempt to control the contagion, and to first-hand witnesses it must have appeared as though people were dropping like flies. Bodies were everywhere. The crowded and cramped nature of the city, with its narrow streets and entranceways, and stacked housing, helped the plague to spread rapidly. Pepys recalled on 15 August meeting 'a dead corps of the plague' in a narrow alleyway. On 7 September John Evelyn, having sent his wife and children to Wotton in Surrey to keep them safe, lamented the sorrowful condition of the city:

> 'Came home, there perishing near 10,000 poor creatures weekly; however, I went all along the city and suburbs from Kent Street to St James's, a dismal passage, and dangerous to see so many coffins exposed in the streets, now thin of people; the shops shut up, and all in mournful silence, not knowing whose turn it might be next.'[4]

Pepys ruminated on the desolation of his city on 14 September, penning in his diary that he had found 'the Angell tavern at the lower end of Tower-hill, shut up, and more than that, the alehouse at the Tower-stairs'. The plague slowed in the autumn months of 1665, but thousands of lives were still lost. By the beginning of 1666 exterior commentators had begun to be hopeful that the coming of cold weather would finally halt the disease. On 26 January Josselin spoke of 'the greatest plague in England since [that] in Edward the thirds time, and yett it continues [...] What God may doe, the weather being now cold frostie, I know not, but hope well'. The city authorities had tried their best to prevent the spread of infection, but with limited knowledge of how the plague was transmitted from person to person they were left to issue speculative orders to London's citizens in the hopes that they would prove effective. Preventative orders published on behalf of the king in 1666 were imaginative, if not wholly convincing. Fires were to be made 'in moveable Pans' for 'all necessary publique Meetings in Churches' and other 'convenient Fumes to correct the Air' were also to be burned; the authorities hoped that this would cleanse the bad air that they believed aided the plague's transmission. Cats, dogs, swine, and pigeons were banned from roaming the streets, and rotten meats, fish, and other flesh were forbidden to be sold in shops and markets. One measure that is likely to have had a positive effect on the stemming of the disease was the shutting up of infected dwellings,

The Diseases and Casualties this Week.

Disease	Count	Disease	Count
Abortive	6	Kingsevil	10
Aged	54	Lethargy	1
Apoplexie	1	Murthered at Stepney	1
Bedridden	1	Palsie	2
Cancer	2	Plague	3880
Childbed	23	Plurisie	1
Chrisomes	15	Quinsie	6
Collick	1	Rickets	23
Consumption	174	Rising of the Lights	19
Convulsion	88	Rupture	2
Dropsie	40	Sciatica	1
Drowned 2, one at St. Kath-Tower, and one at Lambeth	2	Scowring	13
		Scurvy	1
Feaver	353	Sore legge	1
Fistula	1	Spotted Feaver and Purples	190
Flox and Small-pox	10	Starved at Nurse	1
Flux	2	Stilborn	8
Found dead in the Street at St.Bartholomew the Less	1	Stone	2
		Stopping of the stomach	16
Frighted	1	Strangury	1
Gangrene	1	Suddenly	1
Gowt	1	Surfeit	87
Grief	1	Teeth	113
Griping in the Guts	74	Thrush	3
Jaundies	3	Tissick	6
Imposthume	18	Ulcer	2
Infants	21	Vomiting	7
Kild by a fall down stairs at St. Thomas Apostle	1	Winde	8
		Wormes	18

Christned { Males — 83, Females — 83, In all — 166 }   Buried { Males — 2656, Females — 2663, In all — 5319 }   Plague — 3880.

Increased in the Burials this Week — 1289.

Parishes clear of the Plague — 34.   Parishes Infected — 96.

The Assize of Bread set forth by Order of the Lord Maior and Court of Aldermen, A penny Wheaten Loaf to contain Nine Ounces and a half, and three half-penny White Loaves the like weight.

2. An excerpt from the Bill of Mortality for the week commencing 15 August 1665. It lists the many causes of death in the capital at this time in London's history. The Bills had been printed on a regular basis in London since an aggressive outbreak of plague in 1603. They provided a way in which citizens could keep abreast of the mortality statistics stacking up around them, being especially devoured when plague epidemics broke out. The Bill here reflects the large numbers of people who were dying from plague in the summer of 1665, with 3,880 deaths recorded for this week alone.

ideally allowing the sickness to burn itself out in a controlled and demarcated environment. This was bad news for symptomless residents trapped in houses with sick relatives and friends, but good news for the rest of London. The setting up of pesthouses by local officials performed a similar service.

By the middle of the year London was recovering from plague. Shops that were once boarded up had reopened, and the king and his court had made a reassuring return to the city in early February. But the pestilence would continue to rage elsewhere in the country throughout 1666, as it had done since its initial outbreak in London the previous year. The capital city had certainly not been alone in its sufferings. Samuel Newton, alderman of Cambridge, related in September 1665 that the 'Great Danger was alsoe then heere in Cambridge, severall dyeing then heere…and at the pesthouses of the sicknes'. By royal proclamation the Stourbridge fair was cancelled again that year. The antiquary Anthony

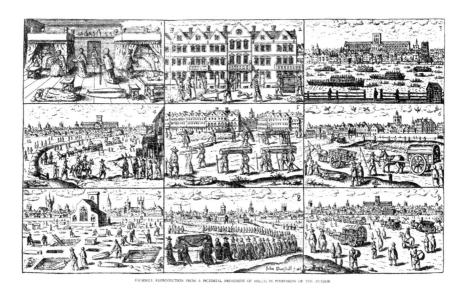

FACSIMILE REPRODUCTION FROM A PICTORIAL BROADSIDE OF 1665 [:6] IN POSSESSION OF THE AUTHOR

3. A reproduction from a broadside printed in c.1665 during the Great Plague of London. At a glance it shows the myriad ways in which plague cataclysmically upended daily life for Londoners. The top left-hand image depicts at least three people reduced to sickbeds in one room. The image below it captures wealthy townspeople attempting to flee the capital, only to be barred from making their escape by an armed party. Across from and below this scene can be viewed the unorthodox burial practices to which authorities were forced to resort as a result of the high numbers of plague dead. Mass graves can clearly be seen in the bottom left-hand image.

Wood conveyed from Oxford in July 1665 that a watch had been set up at night there to 'keepe out infected persons'. The plague had likewise flared up in Chelmsford at this time, being infected by the many 'hecklers' that came to the town from London. A contemporary correspondent observed regretfully that it was not unusual for Chelmsford to be visited by the plague if it had broken out in the capital. The situation did not appear to have improved by October when Betty Adams wrote to a member of the Verney family from Great Baddow in Essex:

> 'The sickness is at Chelmsford a litel mile from me which coseis me to be veri fearfull, so many of our town goes that way to Markit, thos which bee shut up would run About did not sum stand with guns redy to shoot them if they stur.'[5]

Rumours abounded of the plague's spread in the provinces, instilling both fear and disquiet in the preoccupied minds of the English, who could do nothing but wait with bated breath as events took their uncertain course. A dog was supposed to have carried the disease from Wendover to Ellesborough. Local hearsay had it that a pesthouse erected on the outskirts of Aylesbury had been overtaken by fraught sufferers who were burning 'sheep-racks and gates' for fuel. In Whissendine, Rutland, an invasion of traders bringing their goods in the night from an infected town in October 1665 caused the husband of Mrs Sherard to arm himself with a pistol and demand that they be shut up with those who had been foolish enough to receive them. Much further south of Rutland, in Ipswich, the burial register for the parish of St Nicholas exploded with entries in September as the plague bedded down there. By November around 22 plague-related deaths had been recorded in the parish, revealing that in some cases whole families in the town had succumbed to the disease. The Garwoods, the Wades, and the Diers were particularly affected.

By the summer of 1666 the plague had still not subsided. It continued to cause misery in Winchester, where it was thought that 11 people had died in a single day in June. Reports of violence from infected inmates who had been shut up in their houses persisted across the country. In July, further rumours reached the ears of a seventeenth-century correspondent of a violent outbreak of plague on the south coast. Slowly but surely, however, the sickness's reign faltered, and the sickly hubbub that had many obsessed and engrossed began to die away. The Great Plague was the last major epidemic of its kind in England. Plague would never again bring the country to its knees, although other killer diseases would readily take its place in the future. Bubonic plague has a reputation that lingers even to the present day, with many assuming that it was always fatal once caught, that it was the very worst death sentence that an early modern individual could face. It is true that plague was normally fatal, but sometimes people lived to tell the tale. Elias Ashmole remarked airily in 1645 that his maid Elizabeth 'fell sick of the plague, but escaped'.

An epidemic disease that was much more widespread in seventeenth-century England, and that also killed, was smallpox. It is no exaggeration to suggest that most people living in the country at this time either caught smallpox themselves or knew somebody who would develop the condition, be they a vague acquaintance or an immediate family member. It differed from plague in many ways, with an obvious distinction being that it maintained a seemingly constant presence in England from the beginning to the end of the century. A successful vaccine against the disease would not be developed until 1796, leaving seventeenth-century England with an unshakeable problem. Smallpox was a disease that sometimes left people bemoaning the lifelong disfigurements it caused rather than the number of deaths it resulted in. But it was nonetheless greatly feared, and so it should have been, for some estimates have proposed that the fatality rate amongst the infected could be as high as 60 per cent. Ralph Josselin wrote gravely in his diary on 11 July 1674 that, 'the small pox [is] next doore to my house, God preserve mee'. Typically smallpox started with a severe fever accompanied by headaches, lack of sleep, a reduced appetite, and vomiting, before the characteristic spots 'erupted' on the skin, which could be foul-smelling. The appearance of these marks probably confirmed in many cases the presence of the disease. On occasion the infection also caused sufferers to go temporarily or permanently blind.

Smallpox and the long shadow of ill health and death that it cast was a constant blemish on the social landscape of seventeenth-century England. Adam Winthrop of Groton in Suffolk reported in the century's early years, in September 1602, that many of the villagers had fallen sick and died of 'the poxe' there. News came of a 'sad outbreak' of smallpox at Preshaw in 1656. In 1662 the disease 'raged with much malignity and proved mortall to many' at Oxford University, but Anthony Wood was quick to point out that those who allowed physicians to let blood from them invariably survived. The Countess of Warwick, Mary Rich, was 'much affected' in 1668 when she reflected on 'the great mercy of having my family kept from the small-pox, when it raged so much; and that, in the time of my being here [in London], I had not one servant that died'. Edmund Bohun recorded in vivid detail the spread of smallpox through his family in early 1678, and the debilitating symptoms that could accompany infection. On Christmas Day 1677, Bohun was given a warning: his friend John Blome sent him a letter explaining that Mary Brompton, the daughter of Bohun's aunt, had purportedly contracted smallpox, and that while Bohun's son had been staying with them he had shared a bed with the said girl. Edmund was told to be on his guard for signs of infection in his own child. Unfortunately, on 2 January 1678 the disease revealed itself:

> 'The little one fell ill of this disease and was very full of it. On the 22nd, Mary Stiles, one of my servants, fell ill, and was very full. By degrees, however, she recovered.'[6]

A month later Edmund's wife was also ill, although she displayed 'less of the eruption' that pockmarked the faces of his child and maid. The fact that she was pregnant, however, caused her husband to lead 'a miserable life, in the greatest distress of mind and body'. Towards the end of February Edmund himself sickened, and as the disease took hold he believed himself to be more at risk of death than the rest of his bedridden family. He recounted:

> 'I myself sickened, and was in great danger of dying than any other of my family. For nine days I lost the use of my eyes and my senses. For two days I suffered a most violent spontaneous salivation, which exhausted my strength but saved my life. At length, after tossing about in my bed for sixteen days, I rose, more like a skeleton than a man, and as weak as a new-born babe. […] The nurses, at least, acknowledged that scarcely any other person had escaped under the same circumstances. At length, however, I regained my strength, though very slowly, being kept back by fever, pustules in the throat, and other afflictions.'[7]

Edmund had been extremely unwell, but he had miraculously survived. One of his servants, who went on to present with smallpox in March, was less fortunate. Tragically, the stress of seeing her eldest son contract the disease in the same month caused Bohun's wife to miscarry, she having been 'overcome with anxiety and grief'.

The last moments of a patient with a fatal case of smallpox could be nasty. Robert Hooke, the Londoner and renowned seventeenth-century natural philosopher, lost his servant, Tom Gyles, to the disease in the 1670s. In his final hours Gyles was 'pissing blood' and haemorrhaging at the mouth and nose, ending his life in a macabre fashion that most would not wish on their worst enemy. Yet for some in England the horror of smallpox only extended as far as the potential damage done to social appeal, particularly amongst landed gentry circles. Lady Anne Clifford remarked in 1619 that, 'my Lady Suffolk at Northampton House about this time had the Small-Pox', which, 'spoiled that good face of hers'. Even when Lady Anne contracted the disease herself in 1624, having it so 'extremelie and violently' that she thought herself to be at 'deathes Doore', she despaired afterwards that it did 'so marter my face, that it Confirmed more and more my mynd never to marrie again'. Sir John Reresby feared for his daughter's good looks and prospects when she fell ill of the smallpox in 1681, but fortunately, through God's pleasure, she was restored 'without prejudice to her features or complexion'.

The age at which a person died a natural death in seventeenth-century England probably varied according to where they lived, but there was some consistency in terms of the types of illness that people succumbed to. According to the Bills of Mortality, dropsy resulted in the deaths of between 185 and 931 people annually in London during the years 1629-60. It was frequently reported as the cause of death outside of the capital too. In 1672 Oliver Heywood visited a Mr Samuel Mitchel, who was 'lying near death of a dropsy', a swelling of the soft tissues due to the accumulation of excess water. Six years later his 'good old friend' Ellis Bury died of the same complaint. Anthony Wood jotted in his journal that Dr John Lloyd, Bishop of St David's, died 'of a dropsie' in the principal's lodgings at Jesus College, Oxford University, in February 1687. Ralph Josselin greatly feared that the condition would kill him in 1683, complaining that his leg 'sweld wonderfully' and 'issue run out litle'; 'the thoughts of ye dropsie returnd on mee', he wrote, 'God remove the fear of death from mee'.

Agues and fevers were also a prevalent cause for concern, and could be fatal, particularly in small children. Dying from complications of 'the stone' was a common occurrence, the disorder having been made infamous through the accounts that Samuel Pepys provided in his diary of his daily sufferings. Walter Yonge noted the death of the Bishop of Exeter in August 1621, revealing that he had been living with 'seventeen stones in his bladder, and twenty-nine at the neck of his bladder'. Mary Wood was supposed to have died from a complication of the stone in February 1667. Anthony Wood recalled:

> 'She had bin troubled with a paine in her right hip about 4 months before, which at length rising to a head Dr. [Edmund] Dickenson applied a broad plaister of cantharides, as thick as a pan-kake and broader than both a man's hands, to raise a blister. This was one the Monday, Feb. 25; but before midnight it put her to such extreame paine and heated and distempered her blood soe much that all that morning from about 4 to 11 she was greiviously troubled with the heat of the urine which continually came from her, supposed all the while of her sickness by the doctor and those about her to be the stone.'[8]

Attempting to remove bladder stones was a dangerous and sometimes fatal business. Sir Francis Russell, 'being much troubled with infirmities', decided to consult a doctor in London in April 1664 to get to the bottom of his bodily woes, where it was discovered that he was suffering from the stone in the bladder. Russell was given opium for the surgery and two stones were cut out of him successfully, weighing around two ounces each, but afterwards his surgical wound refused to heal and most likely became infected. He died six days after the operation, probably in agony. Pepys underwent surgery to remove a bladder stone in 1658 and survived, against all the odds and without pain relief. He commemorated the procedure's success for many years afterwards with an annual banquet.

'Apoplexy and sudden death', two terms that appeared to be synonymous with one another in seventeenth-century England, was a solid addition to the Bills of Mortality printed in London. For the year 1665, even with plague taking so many lives, there were still 116 deaths recorded in this category, and so too it was mentioned as a cause of death in many other parts of the country throughout the century. Thomas Crosfield described apoplexy in 1633 as a condition that, 'deprives a man of all sense and motion for 48 houres, in which space he is not to be buried: and tho he revive yet never is he perfectly sound'. As twenty-first-century commentators we might interpret this as having a stroke, or possibly a heart attack. Sir Simonds d'Ewes of Suffolk recorded in his autobiography how his friend, Sir Martin Stuteville, had died suddenly at Bury St Edmunds of an apoplexy in 1631. John Rous added some substance to this account, writing that Stuteville had entered a tavern, 'and there being mery in a chayer, either readie to take tobacco, or having newly done it, leaned backward with his head, and died immediatlie'. More commonly acknowledged was a sudden passing that had no apoplectic definition attached to it, with a level of confusion often conveyed as to how an individual could drop down dead without warning. Jacob Bee relayed in January 1684 how Robert Hilton, a justice of the peace in Westmorland, had 'died very suddenly, having been abroad at supper the night before, and went very well to bed the night before'. In 1693 Oliver Heywood noted in his burial register that James Kighly of Thornton 'fell down dead' while digging for potatoes. The burial register for the parish of St Nicholas in Ipswich merely recorded that Rose Barber, a widow, 'died suddainlie' in November 1629.

Cancer was inadequately understood in the seventeenth century and likely to have been misdiagnosed as other ailments in some instances, but it was nonetheless acknowledged as a very real killer by contemporaries of the period. As many as 56 fatal cases were recorded in the Bills of Mortality in 1665. Its slow progression could prove distressing to both the sufferer and his or her loved ones. In 1673 word was sent to Isaac Archer, a Suffolk minister, that his uncle had died of a 'sore in his cheeke', which he supposed 'was a cancer, which began last May, and had almost eaten his whole cheeke away'. Cancer surgery was risky, painful, and very often unsuccessful. John Ward, vicar of Stratford-upon-Avon, reported in 1666 that a Mrs Townshend of Alverston had gone under the knife to have a cancerous tumour removed from her breast. The skin was cut 'cross' by the surgeons and pulled back, before they 'workt their hands' in the tissue and carefully slid the tumour out, which once opened released a 'gush of a great quantitie of waterish substance, as much as would fill a flaggon'. Afterwards one of the surgeons marvelled at the patient's resilience on the operating table, observing that, 'shee had endured soe much, that hee would have lost his life ere hee would have sufferd the like'. Unfortunately the surgery was ineffective and the woman later died, meaning her impressive fortitude was all for nothing.

A committed family member, friend, or servant might take it upon themselves to remove a tumour in the absence of a surgeon. In 1624, William Lilly was willing to do whatever it took to relieve the agonies of his cancer-stricken mistress, who had developed a painful lump in her left breast. As early as 1622 she complained of the discomfort in her breast, 'whereon there appeared first a hard knob no bigger than a small pea; it increased in a little time very much, was very hard, and sometimes would look very red'. Surgeons gave her advice on how to manage the ailment, including the application of 'oils, sear-cloths, plates of lead, and what not', but by 1623 the lump had swelled to a very great size, and was extremely 'noisome and painful'. Lilly recalled that his mistress's pains became so acute that he was sometimes forced to dress the breast two or three times in one night. Eventually he took matters into his own hands, quite literally. Not long before she died, and 'by degrees':

> '…with scissars, I cut all the whole breast away, I mean the sinews, nerves, &c. In one fortnight, or little more, it appeared, as it were, mere flesh, all raw, so that she could scarce endure any unguent to be applied. I remember there was a great cleft through the middle of the breast, which when that fully appeared she died, which was in September 1624.'[9]

It was a drastic act on the part of the servant, but in his view he had been left with little other choice.

The Bills of Mortality catalogued a mass of other natural causes of death in seventeenth-century London, many of which can also be established as common killers in other parts of the country. The annual return for 1665 included 'consumption and tissick', 'spotted feaver and purples', 'griping in the guts', the 'king's evil', 'stopping of the stomack', 'collick and winde', 'French pox', and 'bloody flux, scowring & flux', along with some more unusual entries, for example 'rising of the lights' and 'plannet'. Combined these disorders accounted for the deaths of over 9,000 people in London alone. Writing from Yorkshire Alice Thornton described how her 'mother Gates' died of a 'flux of blood by siege' in 1655, 'as it was suposed to have a veine broaken inwardly, which by fits troubled her many yeares, haveing broken it by a vomit of antemony to strong for her stomacke'. In Suffolk Isaac Archer lost his sister to 'stoppings' in 1664, which resulted in a 'swelling in her face and body' and 'twiddles' under the skin. On 28 April she fell into 'convulsion fitts', with the fourth fit killing her. Archer watched his wife surrender to a similar complaint in 1698. At this time a professional informed her that her 'inwards were obstructed', with pills and drops doing little to improve things, and in September she 'lost her stomach, and had cold sweats'. Death was not far away.

Seventeenth-century England continued to contend with many of the illnesses that had plagued the centuries before it; however, there were a handful of supposedly new natural threats to be dealt with too. Rickets only appeared as a cause of death in the Bills of Mortality from 1634 onwards. It went on to kill 557 individuals in London in 1665. The story was the same for the 'stopping of the stomack', which first hit the headlines in the Bills in 1636 and ended 332 lives in 1665. Thus, the rich tapestry of natural deaths in England was embroidered with new blood-red thread. These, along with every other natural eradicator of the period discussed in this chapter, could make life short, sharp, and sickly for a good proportion of the English population living in the 1600s. Natural death was omnipresent and all too often premature. Although English men and women would have known no different, it still caused vicar Henry Newcome to curse the way of things in 1661:

> 'O the sad things which the Lord sendeth amongst his poore creatures!'[10]

Chapter 2
The Soldierly Death

'But the best way to understand and value the Benefits of Peace, is to consider the Calamities of War; methinks Drums and Trumpets, Carbines and Pistols, Muskets and Canons are Names which sound like to dreadful Claps of Thunder, and Ten thousand glittering Swords seem as terrible as so many flashes of Lightning; for where War is raised, Trade decayeth, Merchants break, Taxes grow High, Mony grows Scarce, Treasures are Exhausted, Laws are Interrupted, Houses are Plundered, Towns and Cities are burnt to Ashes, Corn-fields are Devoured, abundance of Blood is shed, and whole Countries are often laid Wast and Desolate.'[1]

So despaired the English divine Francis Gregory in a sermon of thanksgiving preached at Hambleden, Buckinghamshire, in December 1697. He believed war to be a terrible thing that destroyed trade, sent taxes soaring, encouraged widespread lawlessness, and led to the shedding of much blood, often needlessly. It is true that Gregory would have witnessed his fair share of armed conflict in seventeenth-century England. The 1640s and 1650s were infamously scarred by a destructive civil war, while the period 1652-74 saw a series of fiery naval engagements erupt between the English and the Dutch in the cold waters of the North Sea, known afterwards as the Anglo-Dutch Wars. In 1685 the Duke of Monmouth would incite further violence on English soil in his frenzied quest to dethrone King James II of England, and three years later, in 1688, the Glorious Revolution occasioned yet more pitched battles in England's fields.

War killed extensively in seventeenth-century England, as Gregory was right to intimate in his sermon. A soldier faced the very real possibility in this period of leaving the family home for the battlefield and never again returning, at least not with breath left in him. Furthermore, the fate that awaited a combatant if he did perish in an engagement was often gruesome and unnatural, a far cry from the quiet passing that most non-combatants could hope to enjoy at the end of their lives, ideally in the comfort of their own beds. That is not to say that civilians did not get caught up in the crossfire between opposing forces. A maid might be mortally wounded by a fireball hurled over the walls of a besieged city without any loss of life amongst troops who had actively put themselves in harm's way to defend their territory. In many cases death in conflict came down to simple bad luck, with victims merely being in the wrong place at the wrong time.

The English fought several wars abroad in the early seventeenth century, but such far-removed campaigns would have had very little impact on the day-to-day existence of most of the country's population. The year 1642 brought an abrupt end to this military remoteness. King Charles I sealed the turbulent fate of England for years to come when he made the bold move of entering the House of Commons on 4 January in an attempt to arrest five traitorous Members of Parliament, who, he believed, were plotting directly against their divinely elected sovereign. The act brought to a head more than a decade of ill feeling between monarch and Parliament, and sent the nation spiralling into an internal conflict that would severely deface the country and its stricken inhabitants, bringing death and destruction in unprecedented volumes. Bodies that had once littered foreign battlefields were now piled up outside people's front doors; tortured screams that had until then been carefully muffled behind closed doors and stone walls were now openly shrieked, springing from wrecked streets and bloodied fields. The coming of the English Civil War constituted a monstrous upheaval for civilians and soldiers alike, famously turning brother against brother, friend against friend. Many people died. One estimate has it that 190,000 people perished either directly or indirectly as a result of the war in England, with a further 60,000 dying in Scotland. For the former this equated to a huge population loss of 3.7 per cent, possibly exceeding (proportionately) the loss of life experienced in England as a consequence of the First World War.

The conflict between king and Parliament, the proceedings of which rumbled on well into the 1650s, saw death come in various appalling forms. As expected from an armed conflict, many soldiers died in the thick of fighting. The first major pitched battle, fought at Edgehill in October 1642, was a dangerous and bloody fight that ended in the deaths of around 1,000 combatants and paved the way for a stream of more deadly engagements. The Reverend John Rous commented on the battle keenly from his quiet Suffolk home, relaying, amongst other morsels of hearsay, that two wagons of powder had blown up and killed many on the king's side. A Royalist soldier who experienced the fighting first-hand wrote to his mother after the engagement to tell her with conviction that, 'I do faithfully believe they lost 5 men or 10 of their foot for one of ours besides so many hundred that fled and overrun them', adding that his 'good cousin' Massy was slain in the field.

Under two years later, around 46,000 men were caught up in the largest and deadliest battle of the English Civil War in the unassuming countryside outside York, resulting in 4,000 fatalities. The Parliamentarian Thomas Fairfax recalled the chaos of the Battle of Marston Moor in his memoirs several years after the event had taken place. In a great charge against the Royalist ranks many of his 'officers and soldiers were hurt and slain', with his cornet having both his hands cut, rendering him 'ever after unserviceable', and his brother Charles Fairfax dying later of his wounds. Charles had been deserted by his men in the midst of battle. The Royalist commander, William Cavendish, heard the fight erupt before he saw it, with a 'great noise and a thunder of shooting' giving him 'notice of the armies being engaged'. The first thing Cavendish observed, much to his dismay, was 'the horse of his Majesty's right wing, which out of a panic fear had left the field, and run away with all the speed they could'. He attempted to control the situation and force the frightened troops back into rank, but they fled again and 'killed even those of their own party that endeavoured to stop them'. Throwing himself into the furore Cavendish managed to kill three Parliamentary soldiers with his page's half-leaden sword, but his efforts were to be in vain. The Royalist forces were quickly overcome and lost the battle.

The fatal wounds suffered by civil war participants could be hideous, provoking many of the injured to beg for death. After an early skirmish in Warwickshire in 1642 a dying drummer was found lying with both his arms shot off. Gabriel Ludlow was likewise shot during the Second Battle of Newbury in October 1644, causing injuries from which, unfortunately, he did not die immediately. He was removed from the battlefield and examined by a surgeon, who found:

> '...his belly broken, and bowels torn, his hip-bone broken all to shivers, and the bullet lodged in it; notwithstanding which he recovered some sense, tho the chirurgeon refused to dress him, looking on him as a dead man.'[2]

He was a dead man indeed, as was the Parliamentarian John Hampden, whose pistol burst and shattered his hand at the Battle of Chalgrove Field in 1643.

Just as dangerous for soldiers were the numerous sieges of the civil war. It was reported by the contemporary John Dorney that the siege of Gloucester in 1643 ended with the deaths of up to 50 men, although he was thankful that it had not been more. So many fighters were slain during the siege of Lyme Regis that it was said the water

4. A nineteenth-century imagining of the Battle of Marston Moor, fought near York in July 1644, by John Barker. Marston Moor was the bloodiest of the battles to take place during the English Civil War, killing up to 4,000 soldiers.

serving the town was afterwards 'coloured with blood'. A skirmish there killed many commanders and 'gentlemen of quality', including Colonel Francis Blewitt, whose:

> '...body was found besmeared with blood and dirt, and was caused to be brought from the field into the town on a ladder. [...] In his body appeared three mortal wounds, – two in his back, supposed to be with a brace of bullets out of a musquet, and another in his head.'[3]

The siege of Wardour Castle in 1643 was the backdrop for a particularly horrid death involving a soldier who was buried beneath the debris strewn outside the castle's walls. The enemy refused to dig him out despite the pleas of the castle's inhabitants that he was alive and in need of urgent assistance. His eventual passing came three days later, still buried under the rubble. At Chester, ladders were thrown down and soldiers with them when Parliamentary supporters attempted to mount the city walls to breach Royalist defences in September 1645. As was often the case in the confusion of war, death came accidentally to 27 of the besiegers struggling to storm Pontefract Castle in January 1645. A chance shot from the battlements, or perhaps it was not a chance shot, set fire to the besiegers' own gunpowder supply and blew all 27 men to smithereens.

Civilians for the most part were spared the horror of a death related directly to the fighting, but some were unfortunate. During one episode at the siege of Pontefract Castle, around 50 Parliamentary musketeers were ordered to fire at the fort, killing none but a young maid who was shot in the head while drying clothes in an orchard. She died that night. Soldierly violence led to the death of a daughter of Dr Griffith at the siege of Basing House in 1645, who, spitting insults at the Roundheads as they broke into the fortress, received a fatal slash to the head by an impassioned invader. Perhaps more remarkable are the near misses that were recorded with wonder by contemporary spectators of civil war sieges, where civilians in particular often came within a hair's breadth of death, but were miraculously saved from harm. Three women sitting in the house of Mr Hathaway during the siege of Gloucester were spared a sudden end when a 'granadoe' crashed into the chamber above the kitchen and destroyed the entire room; a piece of it fell down the kitchen chimney around which the women were assembled, but no hurt was done.

Two weeks later 'six great shot' were fired at the town, with a 'twenty-five pound bullet weight' plunging into the kitchen of John Halford. His children had been in the room mere moments before the impact, but by a stroke of good fortunate they had moved elsewhere when the bullet landed.

It has been suggested by some modern demographers that in seventeenth-century Europe no more than 25 per cent of war-related deaths were actually sustained in armed engagements. Disease is suspected to have claimed the lives of the vast majority of combatants who died in service. During the English Civil War, servicemen were faced with noxious living conditions that provided the perfect breeding ground for all manner of unpleasant diseases, most of which were capable of moving through a company with alarming ease and speed. Camps were often dirty, unsheltered, and overcrowded, and the troops frequently undernourished and exhausted, meaning that sickness was unavoidable. Common outbreaks included dysentery, fevers similar to malaria, and

THE SIEGE OF BASING HOUSE.

5. An 1873 drawing of the storming of Basing House by Oliver Cromwell's men in October 1645, following a lengthy siege. As the illustration shows, civilians were caught up in the violence along with soldiers. The daughter of Dr Griffith (perhaps depicted at the centre of this image) was reported to have been killed by a cut to the head.

even plague and smallpox, with typhus and typhoid being the deadliest and most widespread of all visitations. An estimate proposes that the garrison at Newark lost between 240 and 300 of its soldiers solely to typhus from 1643-5. In November 1644 Edward Montagu, Earl of Manchester, bewailed the miserable state of his own regiment, which had been ravaged by fever and flux. Sickness often went hand-in-hand with destitution, only driving the numbers of dead soldiers upwards. Major-General Richard Browne wrote from Abingdon in 1644:

> 'We have 500 fallen sick of late, and one or two being perished for want of clothes have died in the streets.'[4]

For soldiers who ended up being taken prisoner by their enemies, a sickly death, disease being rife in prisons, was perhaps preferable to the fate that befell some of the captured. A friend of Nehemiah Wallington wrote from Oxford on 5 June 1643 to convey the deplorable treatment of detained soldiers in the town, many of whom had been beaten and starved to death by their captors. 'The Rebels to the Parliament prisoners', he penned, 'have equalled or exceeded them in Queen Mary's days'.

Although to the drained soldier, despairing wife, and terrified child it seemed as though the conflict between monarch and Parliament would go on forever, eventually it did subside. Parliament won. The sovereign was executed, and for a while England was governed under a strict and unfamiliar Puritan regime, causing prolonged unrest. Yet the sights of war slowly evaporated from the country's fractured streets and pockmarked fields, allowing for a semblance of restored normality in everyday life. People thanked God that the wretched quarrelling was over.

Even with the reestablishment of peace onshore the English continued to fight wars out at sea, and soldiers continued to die in service. By 1652 commercial competition and naval rivalry between the English and the Dutch had caused a deep rift that could only be settled realistically by the firing of cannons in the North Sea. The First Anglo-Dutch War commenced with the Battle of Goodwin Sands in May 1652 and formally ended with the Treaty of Westminster two years later in 1654, with both sides suffering significantly in terms of lives lost. Being fatally shot at, burned to death, or drowned were all common ways in which a soldier might lose his life while serving on the deck of a warship. At the Battle of the Gabbard in 1653 Admiral Dean of the English fleet was killed by 'one of the first shot that flew from the Hollanders'. Dean's body was seen being covered with a cloak by George Monck, who then proceeded to encourage the startled seamen crowding the ship. The fight that ensued was said to be furious and bloody.

The Second and Third Anglo-Dutch Wars were just as vicious as the first, if not more so. Samuel Pepys eagerly scribbled down in his diary the events of the Battle of Lowestoft in 1665 in the style of some melodramatic pamphlet, including the deaths that occurred that day:

> 'The Earl of Falmouth, Muskerry, and Mr. Richard Boyle killed on board the Duke's ship, the Royall Charles, with one shot: their blood and brains flying in the Duke's face; and the head of Mr. Boyle striking down the Duke, as some say. Earle of Marlborough, Portland, Rear-Admirall Sansum (to Prince Rupert), killed, and Capt. Kirby and Ableson. Sir John Lawson wounded on the knee; hath had some bones taken out, and is likely to be well again. Upon receiving the hurt, he sent to the Duke for another to command the Royall Oake. The Duke sent Jordan out of the St. George, who did brave things in her. […] Admirall Opdam blown up, Trump killed […] all the rest of their admiralls, as they say, but Everson…are killed: we having taken and sunk, as is believed, about 24 of their best ships; killed and taken near 8 or 10,000 men, and lost, we think, not above 700. A great[er] victory never known in the world.'[5]

An account given in a contemporary biography of the Dutch naval officer Cornelis Tromp[6] corroborated Pepys' story, it being written that the Duke of York was wounded in the hand 'with the splinters of the scull of Mr Boyl, and his face besmear'd with the blood of the Earl of Falmouth, the Lord Muskerry, and several of his Domestick servants that were kill'd by his side by a chain-shot from Admiral Opdam's ship'. The goriest encounter of the three wars was fought in 1666 and came to be known as the Four Days' Battle. It was a scene of total carnage, of exploding ships, splintered wood, blood-spattered decks, and men's cries for mercy. Vice-admiral William Berkeley courageously killed 40 men before being shot in the throat with a musket ball, at which point he retreated into the captain's cabin and laid himself down on the table to die. The Dutch later found him 'all over besmear'd with the blood flowing out of his wounds'. Vice-admiral Christopher Myngs was also hit in the throat with a musket ball, according to Tromp's contemporary biography, and stood for about half an hour holding the wound closed with a finger before being mortally shot in the neck by a second. It was posited that he died 'after having given most signal proofs of his Courage to the very last gasp'.

The Battle of Solebay, fought off the coast of Southwold in 1672, saw more lives claimed, including that of the Earl of Sandwich, Edward Montagu. Sir Charles Lyttelton wrote to a correspondent on 4 June claiming that his body had been found at sea 40 miles from the sight of the battle, identified by 'ye George and starr on him'. In his pocket were found a white sapphire ring, a blue sapphire ring, and an 'antique seale' ring, along with a sodden compass. It was supposed that he had leapt off his ship in a desperate attempt to save himself, but drowned

6. A painting of the Four Days' Battle in June 1666, fought between the English and the Dutch off the coast of Kent during the Second Anglo-Dutch War, by Abraham Storck. The chaos and devastation of the battle is clearly depicted in this scene. In the foreground a wounded ship slowly sinks beneath the waves, spilling men into the sea. In the background a scrum of intact ships, including *Royal Prince* and *De Zeven Provinciën*, fire at each other. Throughout the Anglo-Dutch Wars English sailors ran the constant risk of being drowned, burned to death, or fatally shot at.

after the barge he was occupying sunk with the weight of too many men. Tromp's biography naturally approached the event from an optimistic angle, celebrating the heroism of the Dutch and in particular the actions of Captain Brakel:

> 'Captain Brakel did that day, without having receiv'd any order for it, one of the Boldest and most Heroick Actions in the World. For at the very beginning of the battle, whilst the Wind continued to blow still a soft Gale, coming out of de Ruiter's Squadron, followed by a Fire ship, he tackt to the Northward, and fell upon the Earl of Sandwich, Admiral of the Blue Squadron: He made up to him without firing so much as one Gun, enduring all the furious discharges of his Enemy, and of several other English ships that were about him. And when he was got very near the Royal James he fired a whole broadside at her so effectually, that a moment after there was nothing to be heard from her but the lamentable cries of a great Number of poor wounded wretches not to speak of those that were killed with shot or splinters.'[7]

The following year a chorus of lamentable cries was again heard in the waters surrounding Texel, where the English and Dutch fleets clashed in the last major engagement of the Third Anglo-Dutch War. The distinguished admiral Edward Spragge lost his life during the battle along with much of his division. Charles Hatton reported soon after the fight that an accidental shot had sunk the boat he was on and drowned him. A story had it that Spragge's men fastened him to a plank while he was still alive, went away to find another boat, and came back to find a dead body whose head and shoulders were above the water, 'grasping ye planke very hard'.

Death as a result of a sea fight did not always occur at the site of the engagement. Sir William Clarke lost a leg at the Four Days' Battle in 1666 but did not die from his wounds until several days later. Even those watching the action unfold from the supposed safety of dry land were not safe. In 1667 Pepys noted regretfully that a man was killed onshore during the catastrophic Raid on the Medway, having 'laid himself upon his belly' on the opposite side of the river to catch a glimpse of the Anglo-Dutch encounter. A rogue bullet flew from one of the ships and tore up the ground where he lay, ripping apart the onlooker's stomach in the process.

The Anglo-Dutch Wars of the seventeenth century came to an end in the 1670s; the deafening cannons stopped and the acrid smog cleared. By this time it had been 20 years already since the civil war had concluded in England. Peace reigned for a time in the country, and military deaths dropped off. By the early 1680s, however, there were signs that conflict was brewing again. In the latter years of Charles II's reign a new claimant to the throne surfaced, one who was zealously convinced of his status as the true heir to his father's royal title, so much so that he was willing to shed blood for the cause. The Duke of Monmouth was the king's eldest bastard child, and as far as the rules of succession were concerned this disqualified him from ever inheriting the Crown. But the duke would try anyway.

Charles died in February 1685 and was succeeded by his younger brother, James, prompting the Monmouth Rebellion to be launched in earnest that summer. James Scott, Duke of Monmouth, landed at Lyme Regis on 11 June, building an army of poorly equipped men – some only carried pitchforks as weapons – as he toured the West Country in search of military support. Little blood was spilled in the early stages of the uprising. On 16 June one or two men were killed at Bridport, while five days later a skirmish occurred two miles outside of Taunton and killed perhaps 15 or 16 more: three or so from the king's side, and 12 from the ranks of the rebels. Lieutenant Monoux, a commander fighting for the king, was shot in the brain. Although this was, in the grand scheme of things, a fairly mild start to the revolt, King James would be taking no chances when it came to properly arming his troops. On 25 June the storekeeper at Shrewsbury was ordered to deliver to Captain Richard Fowler, for the king's 'immediate service', 40 long pikes, 50 snaphance muskets, 40 collars of bandoliers, and 44 carbines. On the same day the storekeeper at Windsor Castle was instructed to send to Oxford 336 matchlock 'mousquetts', 200 pikes, and 120 'pair pistols with holsters'. If a war was what the duke wanted, then a war is what he would get. The opposing forces finally came face-to-face with one another on 6 July 1685, at Sedgemoor. The duke's followers quickly realised that they stood no chance of winning the battle, for the king's army was far superior to them, both in terms of skill and the sophisticated weaponry the soldiers carried. Many were slaughtered as they attempted to flee the scene. Bodies clogged the ditch separating the two armies and filled a cornfield on one side of the boggy water. Henry Bertie, who had fought for James in the battle, wrote to his brother Peregrine to relate the violent encounter to him, asking that his bad writing be excused because he was composing the letter while still in the field. He explained that they had killed many of the opposing side's men, taken 500 prisoners already, and were in pursuit of more.

Even amongst all the carnage, mercy was allegedly shown to some of the wounded rebels. One man was found lying naked on his back in the hot summer sun, having been there for perhaps 10 or 11 hours in great pain, with a shot through his shoulder and a wound to his belly. The king's soldiers pitied him. He was given clothes with which to cover himself and a stick to aid his walking; he was able to hobble to nearby Weston church, but died that night from his injuries.

The Monmouth Rebellion had failed spectacularly, culminating in what many now believe to be the last pitched battle fought on English soil. A considerable number of men had lost their lives at the Battle of Sedgemoor. Two lesser scuffles in 1688 would see more armed men die in similar circumstances. The English had gladly supported James in seeing off the rebellious Monmouth, but in the years that followed they would gradually turn against their king, weary of his Catholic leanings and ulterior motives. As popularity for the monarch slumped, so admiration grew for the Dutch Prince of Orange, the man who was set to replace him – alongside his wife, Mary, who was King James' daughter. The Glorious Revolution ensued.

The Dutch invaded England in November 1688. James' army was hastily assembled in order to stem the attack, but desertion reduced the king's numbers considerably. The first skirmish occurred at Wincanton in Somerset on 20 November, beginning with the cautious approach of two officers, one from either party, both of whom were unsure of the other man's allegiance. 'Stand, stand, for who are ye?', cried Lieutenant Campbell of the Prince of Orange's forces. 'I am for King James, who art thou for?', replied the second officer, Colonel Sarsfield. Lieutenant Campbell answered that he was for the Prince of Orange. 'God damn mee', the second officer cursed, 'I will Prince thee'. And with that, Campbell is said to have gone boldly up to Sarsfield and 'shot him in at his Mouth and through the Brains, so he drop'd down dead'. Sarsfield's death was, in fact, falsely reported by a Dutch supporter, but it is certain that at this point in the encounter both parties opened fire on each other, killing several men, including Lieutenant Campbell. Hostilities came to a furious head at Reading on 9 December. Some 600 soldiers in the service of the king, mainly Irishmen, clashed with 250 Dutch troops in the town's narrow streets, causing great confusion amongst the townspeople and creating a chaotic atmosphere that allowed the latter to drive James' forces into the marketplace, where they were cut off from all sides and trapped. The people of Reading decided to go on the offensive themselves once the soldiers were reduced to sitting targets, firing at the king's men from the windows of neighbouring houses. The subsequent shoot-off, therefore, probably resulted in the deaths of both soldiers and civilians. It would have been a sight to behold, ending in the clear-cut defeat of James' last supporters. Daniel Defoe described the initial disturbance in a work published in the early eighteenth century:

> 'The first Party of the Dutch found a Company of Foot drawn up in the Church-yard over-against the Bear-Inn, and a Troop of Dragoons in the Bear-Inn-Yard, the Dragoons hearing the Dutch were at Hand, their Officer bravely drew them out of the Inn Yard, and faced the Dutch in the open Road, the Church-yard wall being lined with Musquetiers to flank the Street; the Dutch, who came on full Gallop fell in upon the Dragoons, Sword in Hand, and with such irresistible Fury, that the Irish were immediately put into Confusion, and after three or four Minutes bearing the Charge, they were driven clear out of the Street. At the very same instant, another Party of the Dutch Dragoons, dismounting, entered the Church-yard, and the whole Body posted there, fled also, with little or no Resistance, not sufficient, indeed, to be called Resistance. After this, the Dragoons, mounting again, forced their Squadrons, and entered the Market-place.'[8]

As the goings-on at Reading proved, the widespread civil unrest produced by the Glorious Revolution meant that ordinary men and women also found themselves embroiled in episodes of aggression, sometimes fatally. Anti-Catholic rioting, a form of conflict in its own right, broke out across much of the country in 1688, leading to forceful confrontations that likely ended in civilian fatalities. The lawyer William Longueville wrote on 13 November that the mob had been 'very turbulent' in London that month, with some dying, or at the very least sustaining serious injuries, during the insurrections. He recounted to Charles Hatton:

> 'They have been last Sunday furiously bent for ye destroying that in ye late house of Earle Berkely, and [with] much adoe were beat off, when they had shewed their discontent; but yesternight, as part of ye goods were removing from thence, the said [mob] tooke ye cart and goods and burnt all in Holborne or some other place. Some were hurt and, as 'tis sayd, killed on that commocion.'[9]

The Countess of Nottingham was much perturbed to hear of a riot erupting at Uxbridge on 27 November, between the king's soldiers, often regarded as walking emblems of the Church of Rome, and the townspeople. The unruly troops were said to have set the town on fire in three places, encouraging the inhabitants of Uxbridge to 'rise to defend themselves', which began with the putting out of the trio of blazes, before they turned on the soldiers themselves and killed up to 30 of them. The countess failed to mention the deaths of any of the townspeople, but it is probable that some were killed, perhaps even in their own houses.

James' soldiers possessed a strong reputation for behaving aggressively towards civilians, even if they did not always kill them. In December 1688 the minister of Tylehurston was apparently attacked by James' troops, who stole rings from his fingers 'with the Skin and Flesh', threatened his wife in her bed, and swore to the entire household that they would 'cut them all into pieces' if they were not given money. The chronicler of this episode was convinced that the minister and his family would have been murdered had it not been for the swift actions of a maid, who jumping out of a window had alerted the neighbours to the incident.

War in the 1600s led to personal loss, which in turn caused want. The effects of 'the military death' in seventeenth-century England can be understood most keenly through the many petitions for relief made by grieving war widows struggling to survive without the support of their spouses. Alice Blithe petitioned to the courts in 1648 after her husband was killed at the garrison at Nottingham by a falling gate. With no income to live off, she believed she would starve the same year without the support of the state. Anne Fookes of Halstead, Essex, turned to the state for help after her husband was killed in the service of the Parliament in 1652. It was claimed that she had been reduced to a 'sad condition', was pregnant, and had been relying on the generosity of her friends, who were themselves poor. Worse still was the fate of Anne Bell of Kelvedon, Essex, who was left to provide for four small children after her husband died fighting in the civil war. *The Humble Petition of many Poor Distressed Sea-mens Wives, and Widows* was printed in 1668 and highlighted the plight of widows whose husbands had perished in sea fights in the service of His Majesty. It was declared that many 'are in danger of perishing, and are in great want, and are daily imprisoned; and others for non-payment of their Rent, turned out of their Habitations'.

Death in conflict, or as a product of conflict, was a customary sight in seventeenth-century England, but it was not by any means the usual way of meeting one's maker. It is important to appreciate that war was an exceptional happening, and while it killed considerable numbers when it broke out, it was often absent from the country for extended periods of time, leaving people to die in other more conventional ways. Yet the significance of war in the history of seventeenth-century England means that we cannot ignore the lives that were lost in these various struggles. The terror experienced by so many soldiers and civilians in their final disturbed moments, be it on a body-littered battlefield, in a war-torn town, or aboard a fast-burning ship, must be acknowledged.

Chapter 3

The Criminal Death

'That morning early there was a joyners wife burnt in [Smithfield] for killing her husband. Yf the case were no otherwise then I can learn yet, she had *summum jus*, for her husband having brawld, and beaten her, she took up a chesill or such other instrument and flung it at him, which cut him into the bellie, whereof he died. Another desperat woman comming from her execution cut her owne childes throat, alleging no other reason for yt but that she doubted she shold not have means to kepe yt. The same day likewise another woman poisoned her husband about Algate, and divers such like fowle facts are committed dayly, which are yll signes of a very depraved age and that judgments hang over us.'[1]

John Chamberlain was convinced he was living in wicked times when he wrote about the state of London in 1616. A joiner's wife had recently been burned at the stake for killing her husband, having hurled a 'chesill' at his belly in an apparent act of self-defence, and another woman had slit her own child's throat, believing she could not provide for it and was left with no other choice. One more husband was poisoned to death by his spouse in Aldgate. Things appeared to be just as violent at the end of the century too. *The Cry of Blood: or, the Sin of Murther, Display'd* recounted the murders of three men in a single week in London in 1692, with the author remarking sombrely that, 'it may justly be our Wonder and Surprize, that in a Kingdom Govern'd by such Good Laws, and in a

City Remarkable all over the World, for its Civility and good Discipline, Murthers should yet be so frequent'.

The diverse and crowded nature of London meant that homicide rates were unusually high in the capital in the seventeenth century, while murder narratives undoubtedly developed a dramatic edge to them as they passed like firecrackers from person to person. These considerations can help to account for the ominous reports coming from literate folk such as John Chamberlain and the news-writer Narcissus Luttrell. Most leading authorities on the incidence of murder in seventeenth-century England believe that it underwent a marked decline during the 1600s, in line with the long-established theory that society was becoming more civilised as it entered the early modern period, from about 1500 onwards. The number of indictments and coroners' inquests for homicide and infanticide seen at the Court of Great Sessions in Chester decreased significantly after the 1620s, while in Surrey cases of murder are said to have reduced by over two-thirds in the 80 or so years after 1660. Contrary to Chamberlain's letter of July 1616, in which only female killers were identified, it is thought that a victim was actually much more likely to be killed by a man than a woman in seventeenth-century England. Statistics tell us that four out of every five alleged murderers in Cheshire were men during this period. The story is the same in Surrey, where only one in six accused killers were female.

Acts of murder were very probably on the decline in the early modern period, and seemed to be responsible for very few fatalities in any case, so why single homicide out as a noteworthy cause of death in seventeenth-century England? On this matter the literature speaks for itself. Diaries, pocketbooks, memoirs, and even state papers are full of references to people committing murders. The grisly subject was obsessively consumed and circulated by men and women alike, from all over the country, perhaps for the very reason that it was becoming less commonly observed in the country. By the seventeenth century particularly horrific cases of murder had begun to be printed in specially prepared chapbooks costing no more than sixpence each, complete with enticing titles such as *The true relation of a most desperate murder*, sold in 1616, and *The wicked life and penitent death of Thomas Savage*, flogged in 1680. Homicide was effectively commercialised. The ghastlier the crime presented, the more copies a vendor was likely to sell. Stepping away from this explosion in printed material, however, it is still true to say that murder captured the attention of the literate class in England in a profound way in the 1600s, even if it meant that some only felt the need to comment on a local incident passingly in their diaries.

Being murdered in seventeenth-century England was a risk faced by both young and old. Infanticide – the killing of a newborn baby – was widely committed. At the beginning of the century, in 1603, Adam Winthrop noted with a casual air that one Bridget Horneby had been condemned at the assizes at Bury St Edmunds for killing her 'infant nuely born'. Sixty years later, on 30 January 1662, the vicar Henry Newcome reported that a woman in his parish had been 'brought to bed' of a bastard child the previous night and had almost certainly drowned it soon after the birth, conveying little surprise at the barbarous act. Later still in 1680 a heinous case was described by Oliver Heywood that originated from Dodworth, South Yorkshire, where a servant girl who had given birth in secret in her master's garden then proceeded to bury the infant alive. The harrowing episode appeared to be nothing more than a minor inconvenience for the said mother, who, having abandoned the clothes she was washing to deliver the baby, returned to them dutifully once the deed was done. As these examples demonstrate, the majority of newborn babies killed in seventeenth-century England were done away with by their own mothers, usually because the child had been born out of wedlock, potentially exposing the cardinal sin of pre- or extramarital relations. In Essex, between 1601 and 1665, the mother was held responsible for the death of her child, or children, in 59 out of the 60 cases of infanticide prosecuted at the assizes there, with 53 out of the 62 victims being described as bastards.

The murder of older children or grown men and women was a different kettle of fish altogether. Unlike infanticide, there were many different reasons why an individual might choose to commit homicide, but it was very rarely for the mere sport of it. Murder had purpose. In many cases it was a means to an end rather than a random act of violence, although the death of the victim could undeniably *be* violent. As is still the case in the modern world, money was a major incentive, especially for those who felt as though they had been denied a share. In 1606 a 'papistical young man' from Cornwall killed his father after learning that he would not be inheriting the latter's lands. He perhaps believed that he would be able to procure the lands with his father prematurely out of the way. The desire for revenge may have also played a part. Whatever the motives, the young man was soon overcome with remorse for his crime, for he turned the knife on himself and thrust it into his belly, leading to his own death four days later. The infamous murder of Sir Fulke Greville of Warwick Castle in 1628 occurred under remarkably similar circumstances. Feeling he had been denied what was rightfully his in his master's will, a servant of Greville's decided to respond to the snub in a most violent way. John Rous commented on the scandalous incident from Suffolk soon after it had occurred:

> 'About the beginning of September, came certain newes of the death of sir Fulke Grevill, lord Brooke, of Beauchamp's Courte in Warwickshire, aged about eighty, who had beene a privy councellor in queen Elizabeth and king James his time. The manner was thus: a servant, upon some discontente about maintenance, did in his privy chamber stabbe him about the brest with a knife, but by some rib mist his aime, and then stabbed him in the belly. The lord crying out, he ranne into the next roome and locked the dore, and then ranne upon his owne rapier against the wall; but fayling, he tooke the former knife that lay by his dead maister, and stabbed himselfe therwith, and so died ere any could breake in.'[2]

In fact, Greville died from his wounds four long weeks after the assault had taken place. He was in utter agony, for the cuts had been plugged with pig fat by his physicians and consequently became terminally infected.

Even neighbourly ties could not prevent homicide from occurring when money was involved. A man living in Littleham, Devon, was murdered by his neighbours after they arrived at his house to rob him in 1616, spurred on by the promise of valuable loot. Having committed the act the robbers set the house on fire with the body of the man still inside, which was 'all consumed and burned', save for 'that side where he was wounded, which was neither burnt nor his clothes scorched with any fire, a wonderful judgement of God against murder'. So universal was the committing of murder for financial gain in seventeenth-century England that contemporary commentator Narcissus Luttrell appeared actively confused when Sir Edmund Godfrey, magistrate, was found murdered on Primrose Hill in London in 1678 with his money and watch still in his pockets. Godfrey's was a murder that was never fully explained, although some suspected that it had again been committed out of revenge. The longing for vengeance drove many an embittered soul to take a life, including the 70-year-old Mr Bartram, who in the reign of King James

7. A print from the 1840s, showing the possible way in which Sir Edmund Godfrey was murdered in 1678. Catholic conspirators throttle Godfrey to death with a handkerchief in retaliation for his involvement in the Popish Plot of the late 1670s. His body was later found in a ditch on Primrose Hill, London.

I shot to death Sir John Tyndall, Master in Ordinary of the King's High Court of Chancery, for making 'divers reports against him in Chancery, to the overthrow of Bartram, his wife and children'. Before Bartram could be sentenced he hanged himself in prison.

Domestic tensions led to fatal run-ins between family members throughout the century, encompassing some of the more shocking murders perpetrated. In 1683 Jacob Bee remarked on a 'sad cruel murther' committed by a young man from Durham who was not yet 20 years old, in which his helpless siblings were the victims. The reasons behind the killing spree were not made clear, but the incident played out thus:

> 'When the parents were out of dores a young man, being sone to the house, and two daughters was kil'd by this boy with an axe, having knockt them in the head, afterwards cut ther throts: one of them being asleep in the bed, about ten or eleven yeares of age: the other daughter was to be married at Candlemas. After he had kil'd the sone and the eldest

daughter, being above twenty yeares of age, a little lass, her sister, about the age of eleven yeares being in bed alone, he drag'd her out in bed and killed her alsoe.'[3]

More commonly observed in seventeenth-century England in terms of familial murder was the killing of a wife by her husband, or vice versa, often as a product of trauma experienced in the marriage. However, scholars have concluded that husbands seem to have been much more likely to murder their wives than the other way round. In 1607 two stories emanated from Lincolnshire concerning husbands who had killed their spouses, both of which had been printed for widespread consumption; one involved a man smothering to death his incapacitated wife, while the other told of a husband who had purposefully hit his spouse over the head in an effort to gag her, choosing then to throw her corpse onto the fire 'like a terrible torturing tyrant'. John Brunton, resident of Leeds, claimed that he had murdered his wife by beating her over the head in 1647 because he had feared for his own life. Brunton's wife was by all accounts a violent character, and on the night in question she 'broke open the door with a hedge stake' and 'fell upon him and pulled him down to the ground by the hair of the head'. Adam Sprackling, a drunkard from Kent, had no such excuse when he maliciously killed his long-suffering wife in a fierce rage in the early 1650s, stabbing her in the face with a dagger.

Wives were known to murder their husbands too, sometimes blaming their actions on an abusive relationship. Domestic violence and monetary woes purportedly compelled Margaret Osgood to kill her husband Walter in 1680. One account alleged that on the night of the murder Walter had returned home to his wife drunk, and, after she had struggled to put him to bed, Margaret took the decision to strangle him to death with a piece of whipcord, having first bashed him over the head with a hatchet three times. The motives of some murderesses could be ambiguous at best to external observers. In the 1670s, Oliver Heywood recounted the extraordinary tale of a woman living near Burnley who had put an end to her husband's life by pushing him into a kiln as he was drying corn. She had attempted to cover up the murder by attributing the act to thieves, but the game was up when a few eagle-eyed neighbours spotted blood on her clothes. According to Heywood, a 'wicked filthy confederate' had abetted the accused in her crime, possibly meaning that she had already begun another relationship and wanted rid of her current spouse.

The subservient nature of the relationship between apprentices and masters, or servants and mistresses, in seventeenth-century England rendered murder something of an occupational hazard for bound souls. Letitia Wigington was found guilty of whipping her apprentice to death in 1681, although she denied ever doing such a thing. It was routine for masters to be blamed for the murder of an apprentice even if they were innocent of any wrongdoing. In 1684 William Baker was accused of assaulting one helpless apprentice and murdering another in the space of just two days. Edward Cutbush, the first apprentice, had a chunk of his ear cut off on 20 December 1683, while on 22 December Richard Catt was 'kicked and punched' in 'the head and body', 'inflicting injuries from which he died on 28 December'. Baker was found not guilty on both counts. Sometimes the finger was pointed at both the master and his wife, as in the case of Stephen and Anne Webb, also of Kent, who were jointly blamed for the fatal assault of Stephen's apprentice on 1 January 1684. The 14-year-old girl had been struck 'about the head and body with a staff', dying a month later from her wounds. Again, the Webbs were found not guilty.

The unequal and often unstable association between an apprentice and a master or mistress could occasionally see the former turn murderously against the latter. In 1623 a London apprentice betrayed his mistress by cutting the throats of two of her children in Lombard Street, dubbed a 'fowle barbarous murther' by John Chamberlain. As with so many seventeenth-century killers, the apprentice went on to hang himself.

During the sixteenth century a strange type of formal murder arrived in England from continental Europe. The duel was an Italian import rooted in traditional notions of defending one's honour. It constituted, in essence, a ceremonial encounter between quarrelling individuals, each of whom sought to uphold their reputation by drawing a weapon against their opponent and engaging in combat. The ultimate aim was to walk away victorious with one's honour defended. The contest was widely viewed as a legitimate means of settling an argument in the early modern period, and therefore a participant would only too gladly kill if necessary. Rapiers were the weapon of choice early on in the history of the ritual, but these began to be replaced by pistols as tastes changed and weaponry modernised. By the early decades of the 1600s duelling had become well-established in England, so much so that King James I felt duty-bound to condemn the practice in 1614 in a publication entitled, *A Proclamation against Private Challenges and Combats*. In it he commented on the 'slaughter which we find to have been strangely multiplied and increased of late', an intimation that the duel had resulted in a worrying number of deaths by that time. Yet for many the duel came to be seen as the epitome of gentlemanly decorum, even with its capacity for death and violence, and so its popularity continued to strengthen throughout the century and indeed beyond, allowing the custom to survive well into the 1800s.

Contemporary accounts of duels in seventeenth-century England confirm that they were far from bloodless occasions. Anybody choosing to participate in one would have known that they risked their lives by doing so. Many would not survive the fight. John Chamberlain noted a spate of confrontations in 1610 in a letter to Sir Ralph Winwood, in which at least one person was murdered:

> '…for in one weeke we had three or fowre great quarrells, the first twixt the earles of Southampton and Mongomerie that fell out at tennis, where the racketts flew about theyre eares, but the matter was taken up and compounded by the King without further bloudshed, but the matter was not so easilie ended twixt younge [James] Egerton…and one Morgan a lawiers sonne of goode state: the first beeing left dead in the feild, and the other sort hurt […] The Lord Norris likewise went into the feild with Peregrin Willoughby upon an old reckening, and hurt him daungerously in the shoulder.'[4]

Decades later in 1698, Narcissus Luttrell verified that duels had not become any less ferocious in England, with swords still being used to devastating effect in the name of honour. He wrote:

> 'Letters yesterday from Norfolk brought advice, that sir Henry Hobart was killed in a duel by justice Le'neve: they fought on Saturday, and sir Henry being run into the belly, dyed next day; captain Le'neve was also wounded in the arm: the occasion of the quarrel being, as tis 'said, thus; sir Henry sent Leneve a challenge for spreading a report that he was a coward, and behaved himself so in Ireland.'[5]

The duel was fought on Cawston Heath in Norfolk between Sir Henry Hobart, a Whig politician, and Oliver Le Neve, a country squire. It was

8. A sketch of an early modern duel, dating from 1704. The primary participants are flanked by their 'seconds', who stand watching on either side with rapiers at the ready. The duel was a popular way of settling disputes amongst the privileged classes in seventeenth-century England, but many observers were critical of this formal and ritualised type of murder.

the last recorded encounter of its kind in Norfolk, but was nullified in any case because there had been no witnesses.

On occasion a duel with a definitive ending could leave the losing participant feeling bitter and vengeful, inciting them to commit bloody murder on their victorious opponent in a second encounter. Such was the case in 1676 following a duel between a cornet and a country gentleman in Chichester. Proceedings were conducted in an orthodox manner and the country gentleman managed to disarm his adversary without any hurt done, winning the contest fair and square. The cornet was displeased with the outcome, however, and later that day charged some soldiers to aid him in his quest for retribution. Charles Hatton relayed the story in a letter:

> '...ye cornet left him and went into ye town, called his corporal and one of his soldiers, whom he met in ye streete, to him, and commanded them to follow him; and he went to ye place wher he left ye gentleman, and, finding him ther, commanded the corporal to disarme him; but ye corporal, distrusting his command, he threatned him, and ye gentleman himselfe tooke his sword in ye scabbard, telling ye cornet yt, to prevent his fury against his corporal, he wou'd disarme himself, and yt he looked upon him as a

gentleman who wou'd not doe a base act, and therefore he rendred him his sword, which ye cornet snatched out of his hand and immediately run him through with it, soe yt he dyed on ye place, and ye cornet wase seized on and sent to ye county goale.'[6]

The cornet broke all the rules, and he paid the price for it.

Thus, there was a peculiar system at work in seventeenth-century England. Murder could occur under bewilderingly different circumstances. Some might die from being politely stabbed in the belly with a rapier, on the pretext of a legitimate social confrontation, while others could be murdered barbarously in conditions regarded as being outside the parameters of social acceptability. Of course, in the end mostly all instances of homicide were treated with condemnation, particularly those that were unprovoked or senseless, or at the very least carried undertones of these qualities. Such outwardly indiscriminate happenings made for an uncomfortable atmosphere, conveying a false sense of widespread lawlessness that left contemporaries feeling disturbed. The renowned slaughter of Dr Andrew Clench in London in January 1692 had just this effect on the population. The tale went that the doctor was set upon by two men who had arrived at his house in a hackney coach claiming that a patient was in need of his assistance. Having gone along with them, and suspecting no foul play, Clench was strangled to death in the carriage by the men for no obvious reason, and his body discarded there, giving the crime that wanton edge that so appalled commentators such as John Evelyn and the surgeon Sir Edmund King. Evelyn described it as a 'most execrable murder', whereas King gave ominous details in his account, stating that 'as soone as they had him, they began their villanies; for his hat was found in the street near Barnards Inn, and we believe he was soon dead'. King continued to brood over the case until the end of his letter, declaring it a terrible thing.

The criminal death has a dual meaning when applied to seventeenth-century England. At the same time as referring to death on the receiving end of crime, most notably murder, it can also be an allusion to capital punishment. Although the number of felons who were put to death because of their wrongdoings has been grossly overestimated in the popular imagination for this period, it is fair to say that capital punishment took the lives of a good many criminals throughout the century.

One approximation has it that around 150 individuals per year were victims of capital punishment in early seventeenth-century London alone, which is a figure not to be dismissed. Around 50 crimes were considered punishable by death in 1603, including murder, treason, and larceny. By the end of the century, in accordance with the Bloody Code, this figure had shot up dramatically to around 200, at which time all manner of offences were deemed sever enough to warrant execution. Even with this dramatic rise, however, the number of offenders actually killed by the state tailed off in the closing years of the 1600s. By the beginning of the eighteenth century, it is estimated that as few as 20 people per year in London met their end in this way.

The average murderer, rapist, or thief sentenced to die in seventeenth-century England would in all likelihood find themselves being hauled off to the local gallows to be hanged. Hanging was by far the most common form of capital punishment known in England in this period, and indeed the case was the same in both the sixteenth and eighteenth centuries. The hanging of a criminal was a ritualised process intended to instil fear into the watching masses and deter them from committing felonies themselves. According to Celia Fiennes, writing at the end of the 1690s, the felon was taken from the prison in which he or she had been confined and transported to the gallows in a cart, accompanied by a divine whose task it was to prepare the condemned soul for death. Once on the platform the criminal was invited to address the assembled crowd, who would be watching the spectacle from below. Spectators might be praying or silently weeping, or baying for blood, eager to see justice done. After the dying speech the criminal would be allowed to mutter some final prayers with the minister present, before being asked to forgive the hangman for what he was about to do. Some probably thought it more appropriate to spit in his face instead. At this point the felon would climb the ladder and have the noose fitted around his or her neck, the reality of what was coming finally sinking in. When all was ready the ladder was ruthlessly kicked out from beneath the individual's feet. Because of the lack of force applied, very often this was not enough to break the neck outright, leaving the victim to writhe around on the end of the rope as it slowly strangled them to death. So awful was the sight that it was common for friends or family members to pull on the legs of the thrashing body in an effort to prematurely end their loved one's suffering.

Hangings were mentioned frequently by seventeenth-century men and women, being a part and parcel of everyday life. William Whiteway of Dorchester noted in 1631 how a highway robber at Salisbury was hanged after being condemned for his robberies and throwing a stone at the judge who had sentenced him, knocking the man's cap off, for which he also lost a hand before he arrived at the gallows. On 20 July 1633 Sir Humphrey Mildmay mentioned in passing, almost nonchalantly, that seven people had been hanged at Tyburn for robberies that morning. In 1682 Ralph Thoresby attended a hanging in Yorkshire and remarked on the 'thousands of spectators' who had shown up to witness the death of the accused man, one Holroyd, who had murdered three people, including his own mother. Even in this late year the crowd's appetite for savagery had not waned. They were said to have been 'frustrated exceedingly in their expectations' when Holroyd died 'in the most resolute manner that ever eye beheld', throwing himself off the ladder in an assured fashion without any 'recommendation of himself to God'. The throngs may have been disappointed at the lack of anguish experienced by the felon, but Thoresby himself was left terrified by the display, which was exactly its intention. He reflected that it 'struck tears into my eyes, and terror to my heart, for his poor soul'.

9. Hangings at Tyburn in the seventeenth century, date unknown. Tyburn was the notorious site at which criminals sentenced to die in London were routinely executed.

10. A depiction of women being hanged for witchcraft in Newcastle in 1655, republished in 1796 by D. Akenhead & Sons.

The location of a hanging might be used to add a greater sense of significance to the theatrical exhibition. This was something Sir John Reresby observed occurring in 1682, the same year as Thoresby's distressing experience, when three men were hanged in London in the very street where they had committed their murder. Yet at least one of the men was reportedly not perturbed by the choice, bowing to people as he passed them in the cart and displaying not an ounce of fear as he approached his doom. 'His whole carriage', Reresby noted, 'relished more of gallantry than religion'. Some decades earlier in 1635, Mildmay referred to another man hanged 'where he did his murther', although the killer's response to the chosen location of his death was not recorded on this occasion. Perhaps more distressing for a criminal was being hanged near to where they lived, for this aimed to make the ordeal as upsetting as possible for both the condemned and their relatives. In 1643 Mildmay revealed that such a fate had been inflicted on 'two gentlemen of worth', Tompkins and Chaloner, who were 'hanged near their doors before noon' for their involvement in a plot to subjugate London on behalf of King Charles I. Infrequently people took the law into their own hands when they believed a hanging had not provided adequate justice. After a maid found guilty of murdering her child was hanged at Oxford in 1658 for the requisite period of time, she was taken down by the overseeing bailiffs and miraculously revived by a group of physicians later on that day. The bailiffs were furious. The next evening, just after midnight, they had the woman forced into a coffin, taken to a tree, fitted with a noose, and strung up on one of the branches to finish what they had started. 'Have mercy on me!' she was reported to have cried, but the bailiffs did not listen.

One crime committed in seventeenth-century England was judged far too monstrous and extraordinary to be punished by mere strangulation. A wife who murdered her husband was severely condemned at this time in English history, for in doing so she flew in the face of the natural order of things by revolting against her earthly master. The crime was not homicide but petty treason. In the state's eyes petty treason was deserving of a peculiarly severe punishment. At some point in history it had been decided that burning the murderess alive was the preferred option. The case for such an atrocious punishment was made in a murder pamphlet dated 1677, where the author stated:

> ''Tis but a few years since a Woman near Goodmans-fields was made exemplary, by being burnt to Death for killing her Husband: 'Tis strange if not the Laws of God or Nature, yet that the Severity of the Punishment inflicted in such cases by the Law should not deter all women from such Traiterous attempts; for so it is, for them to rebel against and destroy their Husbands, whom the Institution of God and Laws of the Land have declared to be their Head and Governours.'[7]

Women who killed their husbands, or had a hand in the act, were sentenced to be burned alive throughout the century. A Mrs Brown 'burned quicke' at Bury St Edmunds after persuading an accomplice to murder her husband in 1604. Thirty years later, in 1634, a woman was burned at Smithfield for stabbing her husband in the neck with a knife after they had fallen out at the top of a staircase, which the husband then plummeted down, dying at the bottom 'immediatly'. The following summer, Alice Clarke was duly tossed into the flames in London after it was discovered that she had killed her husband by poisoning him. Although the crime of witchcraft normally came with the penalty of hanging, sometimes it ended with the accused woman being burned alive if, as part of the misdeeds, she had also done away with her spouse. Mary Lakeland of Ipswich was to suffer death by flames for this very reason in 1645. She confessed that, along with bewitching her husband, who 'lay in great misery for a time, and at last dyed', she had sent magical imps to various people to wreak havoc on their lives. In Scotland in 1644 a worse fate was to be exacted on Marioun Peebles, who for the various crimes of witchcraft and murder was sentenced to be 'strangled at a stake at the Hill of Berrie', before being burned to ashes.

Hanging, drawing, and quartering, a famous bygone punishment that tends to characterise the cruel nature of the criminal justice system in early modern England, was reserved for those who had committed the very worst crime: high treason. As the name suggests, this technique involved the felon first being hanged like a regular convict, then cut down and disembowelled while still alive, and finally hacked into four bloody chunks (or quartered). There could have been nothing worse than watching as the executioner tore your insides from out of you, bit by stinking bit. In August 1681 the antiquary Anthony Wood was sufficiently troubled by a local case of hanging, drawing, and quartering to note it in his diary:

> 'At 11 of the clock, Stephen Golledge or College, borne at Watford in Hertfordshire…suffered death by hanging in the Castle yard Oxon; and when he had hanged about half, was cut downe by Catch or Ketch and quartered under the galloes. His entralls were burnt in a fire made by the gallows. He spoke and prayed more than half an hour.'[8]

The high-profile nature of treasonable doings in England in the 1600s means that there are some famous cases to be covered. The failed Gunpowder Plot of 1605, in which a band of disenfranchised Catholics attempted to blow up the Houses of Parliament, ended in the hanging, drawing, and quartering of each of the men who had been involved in the scheme, save for a couple of plotters who managed to escape the ordeal. The first to clamber onto the scaffold and climb the ladder in St Paul's Churchyard was Everard Digby, having first been dragged unceremoniously through the capital's streets for all to see. Those supervising his execution ensured that he was swiftly yanked down from the noose once the ladder had been kicked away. It would not do for him to be dead for the next part. Still alive, Digby was eviscerated and cut up into four pieces, the horror of his death mirroring the revulsion of his crime. The following day, Robert Keyes, another schemer, tried his best to avoid meeting the same intolerable fate. Ignoring protocol, he threw himself off the ladder before the hangman had told him to do so, attempting to break his neck outright so that he might be spared the full torment of a traitor's punishment. He was unsuccessful. Guy Fawkes himself was more fortunate. His own jump resulted in immediate death, meaning that all sensibility was long gone by the time the executioner began the gruesome process of pulling out his entrails.

In the mid-1680s the practice of hanging, drawing, and quartering was still very much in fashion. The rebels who had taken part in the Monmouth Rebellion found themselves facing the punishment as part of the Bloody Assizes. The affair was presided over by the notoriously callous Judge George Jeffreys, who toured the assize courts in the

11. An engraving of the hanging, drawing, and quartering of the Gunpowder Plot conspirators in London in 1606, by Claes Jansz Visscher. In the foreground the condemned are dragged to the site of execution on sledges. Beyond lie the gallows, next to which two executioners are already quartering a conspirator in front of a captivated crowd. One hacks at the body with an axe while the other passes the entrails to a third man behind him to be burnt in a fire.

West Country in 1685 and made it his business to bring to justice as many of the insurgents of the late rebellion as was legitimately possible, all of whom had committed high treason by revolting against their king. It is thought that several hundred men were sent to the gallows over the course of the campaign, which is fewer than is popularly assumed, but is nonetheless a startling figure to modern eyes. A warrant issued to the officers of Bath in September 1685 described the punishment to be inflicted on the rebels who had been condemned in that town:

> 'Whereas I have received a warrant under the hande and seale of the Right Honourable Lord Jeffreys for the executing of several Rebells within your said Cittie. These are therefore to will and require yow immediately on sight hereof to erect a Gallows in the most publicke place of yor said Cittie to hang the said Trators on, and that yow provide halters to hang them with, a sufficient number of faggots to burne the Bowells of fower Trators, and a furnace or cauldron to boyle their heads and quarters, and salt to boyle therewith, halfe a Bushell to each Traytor, and tarr to tarr ym with, and a sufficient number of speares and poles to fix and place their heads and quarters. You are also to provide an Axe and a Cleaver for the quartering the said Rebells.'[9]

As the warrant specified, the rebels' punishment was to go beyond mere hanging, drawing, and quartering, for this alone was too good for them. Their heads and quarters were to be preserved in salt and pitch and then strung up on poles around the countryside as a warning to onlookers, which one can safely assume worked. According to contemporary accounts there was scarcely a tree in all of the West Country that did not have body parts hanging from it in the autumn of 1685. Logic dictates that these reports were a gross exaggeration. The stench, however, was still said to be unbearable, causing travellers to avoid certain routes that were adorned with the putrefying carcasses of men who had tried and failed to overthrow their sovereign. Such morbid displays were a common enough sight in England, and had been since the start of the century. During a tour of England in 1602, Frederic Gerschow, secretary to the Duke of Stettin-Pomerania, espied with trepidation the heads of no less than 30 traitors stuck menacingly atop spikes on London Bridge, their gazes frozen with the expressions they had assumed at the moment of their deaths. The prime position of those heads was no accident. The whole of London needed to see, digest, and understand what happened to a person when they had the nerve to betray the realm.

Continuing with the theme of severed heads, it is interesting to note that the very first 'rebel' to be condemned for participating in the Monmouth Rebellion was in fact beheaded. Lady Alice Lisle was hauled before Jeffreys at Winchester for harbouring two men who had fought for Monmouth at Sedgemoor. In sheltering the rebels she herself was branded an enemy of the state, although during the trial she profusely denied any personal support for the uprising. Jeffreys bullied the jury into arriving at a guilty verdict and Alice was sentenced to be burned at the stake for her crime. This was mitigated to beheading by James II on the grounds of her social rank. On 2 September 1685, Lady Lisle, an old woman of around 70, was led out of The Eclipse Inn on Winchester's market square and escorted to the waiting block. The dying speech was an important part of execution etiquette, and so she was supposed to have delivered the following address, beginning with:

'Gentlemen, Friends and Neighbours,

It may be expected, that I should say something at my Death, my Birth and Education being near this place.'

She continued by justifying her actions, forgiving those who had wronged her, and thanking the king for reducing her sentence to decapitation:

'The Crime was, my Entertaining a Non-Conformist Minister, which is since sworn to have been in the Duke of Monmouth's Army. I am told, if I had not Denyed them, it would not have affected me: I have no Excuse, but Surprize and Fear; which I believe my Jury must make use of to Excuse their Verdict to the World. I have been told, That the Court ought to be Council for the Prisoner: Instead of Advice, there was Evidence given from thence, which (though it was but Hear-say) might possibly affect my Jury. My Defence was such, as might be expected from a Weak Woman; but such as it was, I never heard it repeated again to the Jury. But I forgive all persons that have Wronged me; and I desire that God will do so likewise. *I* for give Coll. *Penraddock,* although he told me, *He could have taken those Men before they came to my House.* […] I acknowledge his Majesty's Favour in Revoking my Sentence; and I pray God he may long Reign in Mercy as well as Justice, and that he may Reign in Peace, and that the True Religion may Flourish under him.'[10]

Other reports maintained that due to her advancing years she said very little at the block. Whether she spoke before the end or not, the executioner's swing inevitably followed. The country at large judged Jeffreys' apathetic attitude to be unacceptable, and Alice's death was widely denounced.

Beheading as a form of capital punishment was a courtesy awarded to the few and not the many. Condemned men and women of noble birth were granted this sentence because it was usually quick and painless, and therefore befitted their genteel status. Decapitations were huge events in seventeenth-century England. Part of the reason for their popularity was the element of celebrity involved in each execution, for they often involved a famous name, although the average labourer or maid might just want to see a good piece of head-hacking. Sir Walter Raleigh's execution in 1618, for instance, drew vast crowds. The celebrated explorer had dodged the block one too many times when he was ordered to be put to death for conspiring against James I in the October. A testament to his resolve, he remained level-headed on the scaffold at Whitechapel on the morning of 29 October and urged the multitudes surrounding him to do nothing to defame their king. Just before the end, he took off his doublet and asked the executioner to show him the axe, allegedly saying, 'dost thou thinke that I am afraid of it?' He clearly wasn't. Having forgiven the executioner, Raleigh laid his neck on the block and indicated that he would lift his hands when he was ready for the fatal blow. His head came off after no more than two strokes. It was shown to the crowds on each side of the scaffold and put into a red leather bag, his sumptuous gown thrown over it.

The Duke of Monmouth faced a less straightforward experience at his own beheading in 1685. Unfortunately for him, the promise of a fast and clean finish on the block was never fully realised. His last few days were luckless from the very start. In the first place, the great pretender to the English throne had been captured while hiding in a ditch dressed in shepherd's clothes, against all the odds. His execution was a continuation of this misfortune. So infamous was Monmouth and his failed rebellion that he was treated to a traitor's death on Tower Hill on the warm morning of 15 July. Four ministers accompanied him to the scaffold, but no amount of prayer would be able to save him from the botched job that was coming. Some might say it was evocative of his botched revolt. The Verney correspondence includes a description of the execution:

> 'The Executioner had 5 blowes at him, after the first he lookt up, & after the third he put his Leggs a Cross, & the Hangman flung away his Axe, but being chidd tooke it againe & gave him tother two strokes; and severed not his Head from his body till he cut it off with his Knife. This Joseph told me…I mett him coming from Tower Hill, where he saw the Execution done.'[11]

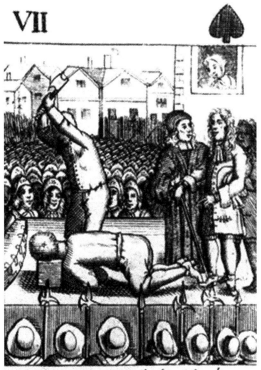

The late D of M beheaded on Tower Hill 15 july 1685

12. A seventeenth-century playing card capturing the moment James Scott, Duke of Monmouth, is executed at Tower Hill on 15 July 1685. The executioner can be seen in mid-swing as countless onlookers swarm around the scaffold. Some say it took five blows to severe the Duke's head from his body, which is ironic considering that beheadings were designed to be quick and painless.

IACOBUS, HARTOG VAN MONMOUT,
Seer Elendiglyk het Hooft afgeslagen .

13. A Dutch etching from 1698 showing the botched beheading of James Scott, Duke of Monmouth. The etching is by Jan Luyken.

After five excruciating blows the Duke of Monmouth's head finally came off. It appears certain that he would have been aware of at least the first couple of swings.

King Charles I's execution in January 1649 has to be the most famous beheading of them all to occur in seventeenth-century England.

The event was matchless in terms of its sheer uniqueness and scale, and had many people questioning the very foundations of the country's criminal justice system. How could a nation be allowed to kill its ruler? On what grounds could this possibly be allowed? In the wake of the English Civil War anything seemed possible. The charge brought against Charles Stuart on 20 January was as follows:

> 'That the said Charles Stuart, being admitted King of England, and therein trusted with a limited Power, to govern by and according to the Laws of the Land, and not otherwise; And by his Trust, Oath, and Office, being obliged to use the Power committed to him, for the Good and Benefit of the People, and for the Preservation of their Rights and Liberties; Yet nevertheless, out of a wicked Design to erect and uphold in himself an Unlimited and Tyrannical Power, to rule according to his Will, and to overthrow the Rights and Liberties of the People; Yea, to take away and make void the Foundations thereof, and of all Redress and Remedy of Mis-government, which by the fundamental Constitutions of this Kingdom were reserved on the People's Behalf, in the Right and Power of frequent and successive Parliaments, or National Meetings in Council; He the said Charles Stuart, for Accomplishment of such his Designs, and for the protecting of himself and his Adherents in his and their wicked Practices, to the same End, hath traiterously and maliciously levied War against the Parliament, and the People therein represented.'[12]

Charles was a dead man. The system had gone against him and now the king was going to pay for his war crimes. The evening before his execution Charles bid an emotional farewell to his two youngest children, Henry, Duke of Gloucester and Princess Elizabeth, both of whom cried as soon as they saw him. He gave each child small tokens to remember him by and then dismissed them. After that came the longest night of his life, no doubt punctuated by visions of the following day, of the executioner's swinging axe and the awestruck, disbelieving crowds, but hopefully calmed by profuse prayer. When morning arrived it was legendarily cold, prompting the king to put on two shirts underneath his doublet lest anybody should think he was shivering with fear. Charles was then escorted to Whitehall; at roughly 2.00pm he was led through the Banqueting House to the waiting scaffold, which was draped in black cloth. The mass of soldiers encircling the platform was so deep that the king quickly realised it would be futile to attempt to address the watching hordes beyond the pikes. They were too far away for him to be heard. Instead, he spoke to the solemn actors playing their various roles on the scaffold, including the Bishop of London, William Juxon. Once he had said his piece, and with the aid of Juxon, Charles fitted his silk nightcap on his head and tucked his hair away to give the executioner an unobstructed view of his neck. Accounts suggest that he feared the pain that might be caused by the axe's blow, but in his final moments he was assured that the ordeal would be over before he knew anything about it. Charles at last laid his neck on the block and asked the axeman to hold fire until he gave the signal that he was ready to die. The signal was given, and the axe fell, severing the head from the body in one stroke.

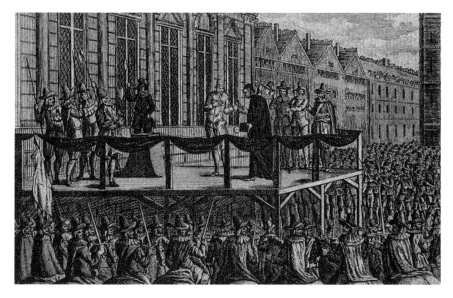

14. An impression of the final moments before Charles I's execution on 30 January 1649. The king can be seen handing over personal items to Bishop William Juxon on the scaffold, with the handsome Banqueting Hall visible in the background, to the left of the scene. A mass of soldiers surrounds the wooden platform and stops members of the watching public from getting too close to the beheading. Spectators are shown lining the windows and even roofs of nearby houses to catch a glimpse of the unprecedented spectacle.

The clergyman Philip Henry later recalled the moment at which the king was decapitated. He wrote, 'the Blow I saw given, & can truly say with a sad heart; at the instant whereof, I remember wel, there was such a Grone by the Thousands then present, as I never heard before & desire I may never hear again'. These were moving words, and regardless of their legitimacy, it is hard to imagine the crowds not reacting soberly to such an unthinkable occurrence. Henry went on to remark that as soon as the head had been removed from the flaccid body, soldiers descended on Whitehall to stem the ensuing chaos. The beheading had caused alarm and anger in equal measure. John Evelyn, a staunch Royalist, was enraged. 'The villainy of the rebels...to try, condemn, and murder our excellent King...struck me with such horror that I kept the day of his martyrdom a fast', he recollected.

Capital punishment was a staple of ordinary life in seventeenth-century England. It was certainly not on vivid display constantly, but the theory at least was ever-present, informing the nation's opinion on what was normal and acceptable and what was by default offensive. It would be tempting to conclude that the country had an appetite for violence in this period, or that individuals were much more hardened to gory spectacles than we are now in the twenty-first century. There is probably an element of truth in the latter if not the former. John Chamberlain imparted one curious seventeenth-century attitude when he observed that, at the execution of three dear-stealers at Hyde Park Gate in October 1619, it was not the strangulated criminals who were most pitied, but, 'a poor labouring man...hired for sixpence to hold their dogs and bear them company to the gallows'.

Chapter 4

The Deathbed

In 1635, John Evelyn's mother lay dying of a malignant fever at the age of 37. She asked that her children be around her in her final moments. To each of them she gave a ring with her blessing, along with careful instructions on how to lead a devout life in keeping with the tenets of Christianity. Satisfied that she had counselled them adequately, Mrs Evelyn then took her husband by the hand and entrusted her children to his care, all the while ensuring that her manner was pious and dignified. The servants were called too, and more pearls of wisdom imparted to them. On 29 September, at 8.00pm, the matriarch finally slipped away, assured that her work was done.

Eleanor Evelyn's passing demonstrated just how important a space the deathbed occupied in the ritual of existence in seventeenth-century England. Crucially, it was the point at which a person reaffirmed their faith in preparation for eternal life with God. It was also where farewells between family members and friends were exchanged. Last-minute counsel was often provided by the dying man or woman to those who were considered in need of it, and directions were customarily given in terms of what should happen to the sick person's worldly goods when they were gone – most importantly, who got what. The deathbed constituted the sombre stage on which all of these acts played out, and to fulfil each of them, or even just some of them, was considered the best end attainable. At this closing moment in an individual's life, whether it had been long or short, there was a patent clash between the earthly and the divine. God was waiting expectantly in the heavens, but loved ones were being left behind in the mortal world, and so both parties required consideration.

Most contemporaries of Eleanor Evelyn strove to accentuate their piousness on the deathbed in anticipation of the afterlife, just like she had done in Wotton in 1635. The vicar Matthew Henry noted two deathbed scenes in 1695 in which the dying individual was predominantly concerned with preparing their soul for heaven, revealing the strength of devout preoccupations even at the end of the century. Mr Becket, chaplain to the daughter of the Earl of Chesterfield, 'finished well' in March. He conveyed to Henry that he was ready and willing to die a Christian death as he lay sick of a consumption, and, even though speech became difficult towards the end, he instructed all those around him to 'prepare to follow him to the glorious mansions above'. Becket was only 25 years old when he passed away, but nobody could deny that he had mastered the art of a good death, least of all Henry. In April, John Wilson of Warwick also died of a consumption. His own conduct was impressively reverent on the deathbed, for he repented of his sins amongst other religious acknowledgements. Henry wrote afterwards that:

> 'He lay for some time before he died in raptures of joy. He said he could, through grace, stand upon the brink of one world, and look into another without any amazement; that he had, indeed, had some struggles in his soul, but he had endeavoured to deal roundly with himself, in renewing his repentance; and now he had boldness to enter into the holiest through the blood of Jesus.'[1]

Wilson epitomised the common desire to show no fear in the last moments of life in the early modern period, for only then could true Christian resolve shine through. When George Savile, Marquess of Halifax, found himself close to death in the very same year, he made every effort to uphold a Christianly boldness that would score him valuable points in the next world, even in the face of grave sickness. The ordeal he went through was remarkable. One evening, against the advice of his wife, George ate an undercooked chicken that he was said to have enjoyed very much. He went to bed that night feeling quite well. By the next morning, however, he was vomiting heavily. The heaving was violent and caused his gut to rupture. He had not passed a stool for several days prior to this, so his gut was filled with a large quantity of hard excrement that made it impossible for his physicians to successfully deal with the problem. The ruptured gut was left to fester and soon turned gangrenous, meaning that George's sickbed transformed into his deathbed in very little time. The affliction with which he had to deal would have left him in horrendous pain: without the aid of effective pain relief, infections could be incredibly painful to the sufferer. The Marquess also had to go through the unenviable ordeal of having a piece of his insides hanging out of him, disturbing both visually and in terms of the awful smell issuing from the wound. Yet his religious duties were never far from his mind in his final breaths. Even when confronted with a throbbing and stinking infection, George received 'ye sacrament' very devoutly, after which he expressed with 'great Christian piety' his 'resignation to ye will of Heaven'. A brave soul indeed.

A second characteristic feature of the deathbed scene was the presence of kin, including neighbours, which performed a religious function as much as it did a social one. A family member might be in attendance at the bedside to bid farewell to their beloved, quite understandably, but they were also expected to provide godly aid and comfort to the sick individual as they faced their final test of strength before ascending to 'the glorious mansions'. Accounts would appear to suggest that a good proportion of those who showed up at the deathbed did so simply because they wanted to say a final goodbye, being driven by raw emotion alone. Any religious obligations were firmly placed in the subconscious. Likewise, relatives were actively summoned by the infirm for the same end. Hearing of the imminent decease of his sister Cecilia, Simonds d'Ewes 'hasted on foot' to her deathbed with his two elder sisters in 1620, so eager were they to see and speak to her before she died. This entailed crossing London in the middle of a fierce blizzard, with the ground 'cold and wet underfoot'. When Catherine Aston's husband, Herbert, a Staffordshire gentleman, came to her sickbed at 3.00am in 1658 and found her feverish and short of breath, he dismissed the watcher at once and sat with her instead, fearing that she was not long for this world. Mrs Aston herself called her children to the bedside when she realised the end was close. 'Pray Mr Aston let me see all the children', she whispered, 'you know not how soon I may die'. She wanted to say goodbye to them. First giving them all her blessing, as Eleanor Evelyn had done, she then told them always to be good, and to do whatever their father asked of them, and urged the older children in particular to remember her words. After this she 'affectionately' gave each child a kiss, 'bad God bless them', and dismissed them.

Isabella Twysden of Kent was much consoled by the knowledge that there were six people with her father Sir Nicholas Saunders when he lay on his deathbed in February 1649, including his son. Yet she was nevertheless deeply distressed that she herself was not able to be with him as he died. There were some, though, who possessed a different mindset. Samuel Pepys couldn't bear the thought of being in the same room as his brother when he passed away in March 1664. At 8.00pm, when Thomas Pepys had fetched up so much phlegm that his breath had started to come in rattles, Pepys excused himself from the deathly scene and left the house, having 'no mind to see him die'. Upon his return mere minutes later, his brother was dead. He wrote in his diary:

> 'I went up and found the nurse holding his eyes shut, and he poor wretch lying with his chops fallen, a most sad sight, and that which put me into a present very great transport of grief and cries, and indeed it was a most sad sight to see the poor wretch lie now still and dead, and pale like a stone.'[2]

This kind of attitude was rare, in the sources that have survived from the period at any rate. Nobody can refute the pain involved in seeing a person die, of course, and even in a world where death was more visible it is probable that there were other people just like Samuel Pepys who felt unable to perform their social responsibilities when the time came to do so. That said, in the majority of cases attendance at a deathbed was seen as an opportunity by kin in seventeenth-century England, not a trial that one should avoid. In 1673, Elias Ashmole appreciated that visiting a Dr Wharton on his deathbed provided the opportunity for the two to be reconciled, considering the differences that had 'formerly fallen out' between them, and Dr Wharton acknowledged the same.

Alongside family members, friends, and neighbours, it was common to have a priest in attendance at the deathbed, who might pray with the ailing individual, offer spiritual words of guidance, or administer Holy Communion. This last act was frowned upon by Puritans, who believed it stank of the last rites associated with Catholicism, an outlawed branch of Christianity in seventeenth-century England. The minister Oliver

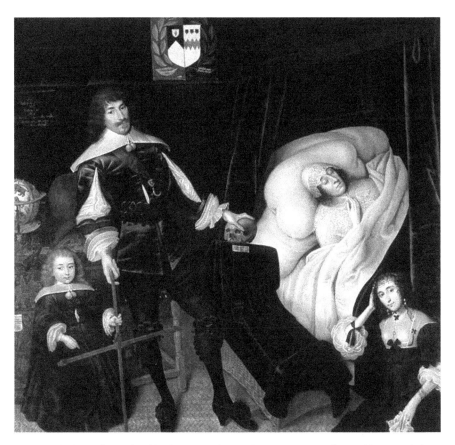

15. A painting of the deathbed scene of Sir Thomas Aston's first wife, Magdalene Poulteney, by John Souch, c.1630s. The deathbed occupied an important space in the ritual of existence in seventeenth-century England. It was the point at which a person reaffirmed their faith in preparation for eternal life with God. It was also where farewells between family members and friends were exchanged.

Heywood's diaries, spanning much of the second half of the century, are full of references to visits he made to the dying in and around Halifax. In April 1668 he was called to the deathbed of John Massey, who proclaimed with exasperation, 'here's a faithful minister of Jesus Christ' on Heywood's arrival at his side. Oliver then sat and prayed with the man. It was not always an easy task. In January 1681, having already visited the patient three times, Heywood sat and prayed with an incapacitated victim of liver disease for two or three hours as he bled violently from the mouth and gasped for air. He expired while Oliver was still with him. Even if Heywood could not be physically present at a deathbed, kin might still travel to him to ask that he pray for their soon-to-be departed loved one from afar. The minister was called down from an upper room of his house in 1700 because two women had turned up at the front door requesting that he pray for the dying wife of one John Crowther. He agreed to help, and said prayers for the woman with his family after dinner that evening.

One had to place a level of trust in a priest who sat by the bedside of a person close to death, particularly if they were left alone for extended periods of time. Sometimes that trust was misplaced. One of the charges made against Edward Finch in 1639, who was vicar of Christ Church in London, concerned his questionable conduct while attending to a dying woman in his parish. In the first place, he was so drunk while administering Communion to her that he forgot how the order of service went. He then neglected to recite the Lord's Prayer. What came next, however, was far more sinister:

> '(Charge) That at the same time he caused all present with the said woman to depart the room, and then enjoined the sick party to confess unto him all her secret sins. [...] That, being so alone with the said woman, he demeaned himself so uncivilly...that she was fain to cry out for her husband to come in.'[3]

Finch was either too drunk to be aware of his abuses or simply impervious to them, for afterwards he considered that he had provided a good service and demanded a fee of three shillings fourpence. When the Grand Committee for Religion sat in 1641 and considered his crimes, they found him guilty of every one of them.

The unfortunate circumstances surrounding all too many seventeenth-century deaths reduced some deathbed scenes to troubling episodes that were in stark contrast to the calm and Christianly occasions heretofore described. Royalty were not exempt from such bad luck. In 1667 the Countess of Warwick visited the Duchess of York, Anne Hyde, whose children were both seriously ill and bedridden. She found one of them, Charles, in a 'convulsion fit' and close to death. It was a scene of emotional chaos. The women in attendance shrieked at the four doctors present to give the boy something to ease his discomfort, but they could provide nothing of adequate use, and so he was left to die in writhing agony. Mr Banister

Hulme left the world in a similarly upsetting way near Manchester in 1673, at the age of 17. He returned home to his parents from school one day and complained of a pain in his head, which by nightfall had turned into projectile vomiting. Doctors were sent for, but to no avail. Banister lay on his deathbed in a most unnerving manner, growing 'frantick', 'singing much', and throwing himself around to such an extent that four grown men could not hold him down. The physicians were unable to work out what ailed the adolescent, and so it was in this manner that he died. There was no mention of any exhibition of Christianly resilience in this instance, while it seemed equally doubtful that Banister's parents would have provided much comfort to their disturbed son at the bedside.

Giles Moore, rector of Horsted Keynes in Sussex, recorded that his brother managed to utter a few prayers directly before his expiration in 1670, exuding some Godly steadfastness in doing so, but it remains to be seen whether this would have made up for the frenzied deathbed antics that came before them. At the beginning of the illness a surgeon from Newport felt sure that the man was not in danger of death. 'Sir, if you be in a dying condition I am as much mistaken in that as I ever was in my life', he was quoted as saying. The following morning he repeated the assertion, reassuring the patient that, 'God hath designed you for a longer life'. Alas, it became clear soon afterwards that the surgeon had read the situation erroneously, and that Giles' brother was in fact dying. Any bed he occupied was now for all intents and purposes his deathbed, and the days he had left were characterised by the fact that he was 'on the deathbed'. The end of his life turned out to be strange, harrowing, and somewhat eccentric. It can be stated with a fair degree of confidence that the man was suicidal right up until he died of natural causes. As he began to weaken and fade in his chamber he complained that he was miserable and in unbearable levels of pain. A day later, while the servant waiting on him was absent from the room, he took his chance to end it all; he ran downstairs and threw himself into a well. The radical performance must have been witnessed by members of Giles' household, for no sooner had he plunged into the water than he was pulled out of it again and returned to his warm bed, where he purged naturally. The brother became restless after this. He moved from bed to bed, or deathbed to deathbed, being unable to find the comfort he so desperately craved, and continually feeling unsatisfied. A sense of calm only descended in the last moments of his life.

From mayhem to mysticism, some beheld the deathbed as a numinous arena in which strange happenings occurred, reflecting the superstitious proclivities of deeply spiritual men and women in England in the 1600s. Witnesses were adamant that they had glimpsed extraordinary sights in the vicinity of a dying person, with perplexing reports surfacing from every county. In Yorkshire in 1670, Oliver Heywood claimed that while he had been keeping vigil at a sick child's bedside one night, the flame of a candle burning in the chamber had turned blue several times and then blown itself out, all before his very eyes. 'I thought it strange', Heywood commented, 'and looked upon it as an emblem and presage of death'. Charles Lyttelton wrote to Charles Hatton in January 1692 to convey the odd spectacle that had been witnessed as Katherine Jones, Viscountess Ranelagh, lay dying the previous December in London. A flame had erupted out of one of the building's chimneys for no discernible reason. Perhaps not unexpectedly, even the dying themselves described peculiarities from time to time. Before death took him in 1685, John Borrow of Durham told those around him that he had seen 'a coach drawn by six swine, all black, and a black man sat upon the cotch box'. An omen of death, no less. It was believed that the vision led directly to his passing.

Among its other incarnations, the deathbed resembled something of an administrative epicentre in seventeenth-century England. An overwhelming percentage of seventeenth-century testators chose to compose their last will and testament while occupying it. We are made aware of this to a certain extent in contemporary accounts, but it is most discernible through the surviving wills themselves. The majority of these documents expressed in the opening few lines that the testator was 'sick in body' at the time of the will's drawing up. The prevalence of last-minute will-making is easy enough to explain: it only occurred to testators to draw up a will when they realised their decease was imminent. Although the deathbed performance of Giles Moore's brother went against the recommendations of most manuals written on the subject when it played out in 1670, the man did at least have the good sense to consider his will as soon as he realised he was sick. On 2 August he moved into the back rooms of the house and summoned Giles to him, declaring dramatically, 'Brother, I am a dead man', before revealing that he was worth £4,400 and proposing to leave his entire estate to his male sibling. The esquire Edmund Bohun visited his sick cousin in September 1680. Discovering that the said cousin had no will, Edmund urged him that now was the time to make one. The cousin refused at first, but the esquire was persistent, listing the many credible arguments in favour of getting one's affairs in order if one was unwell. The cousin finally gave in. Dame Ursula Verney had already written her will by the time she found herself on her deathbed in 1668, so she instead took the opportunity to make some eleventh-hour adjustments. A legal professional listened intently from the bedside as Ursula attempted to recite her alterations, but in the end nobody could fathom her words, for she was breathing too hoarsely to be understood.

Whether testators drew up their wills on the deathbed or beforehand, the majority of the documents remained strictly formulaic in nature, sharing common features that extended from one end of the century to the other. They almost always began with the religious acknowledgement 'in the name of God Amen'. The opening sentences habitually stated the date on which the document had been written, the name of the testator, their place of residence, and a declaration of occupation or rank. As has already been mentioned, comment was also frequently made on the health of the testator. Many announced that they were sick or weak, but crucially whole in mind, while a smaller proportion proclaimed with pride that they were in good health at the time of will-making. Religious preambles were a standard insertion throughout the seventeenth century. These were often similarly phrased, reflecting the generic quality of the content found in wills in this period. More intrinsically, however, the preambles reiterated the religious significance of the will-making process. Typical expressions that made up the religious preamble of a will included hope of salvation and references to the resurrection of the body. Sir John Croftes of Little Saxham, knight, had the following preamble in his will of 1627:

> 'I comitt my soule into the handes of my deare and blessed Saviour Christ Jesus, by vertue of whose death and sufferings alone, and by not other meanes or merritt of my owne being a sinnfull creature, I doe steddfastlie believe I shall stand cleare before him from all my sinnes…and that att the last daie my soule and bodye shalbe reunited togeather againe, and then be made partaker of that glory in heaven.'[4]

Croftes' preamble described how he was committing his soul to Christ in anticipation of the Resurrection. The rest of the content of a will was dependent on the testator's circumstances. Directions could be given on the distribution of a whole variety of things: household items, animals, pieces of land, trade equipment, personal valuables, and even clothing. Croftes' will, for instance, discussed the distribution of land. Place of burial requests usually came after the religious preamble, but other funeral, burial, and remembrance wishes might appear anywhere in the will. The text normally ended with the appointment of an executor, charged with overseeing that the testator's instructions were faithfully executed after they had died, a supervisor or supervisors, tasked with assisting the executor in his or her duties, and the naming of the will's witnesses. Chosen executors were typically spouses, children, or friends, being individuals who the testator could implicitly trust. Finally, date of probate came at the end of wills that had been proved in court.

As literacy rates rose towards the end of the century, so too did it become more common for testators to pen their own wills. As a rule, however, wills in this period were more often than not dictated to a scribe, particularly if the testator was on their deathbed. To take the scribe Ralph Tailor of Newcastle as an example, in 1636 he alone wrote at least a quarter of the surviving wills made by plague victims in the city. It is occasionally possible to ascertain beyond doubt if a will that has survived was the work of a scribe or the testator. John Lany of Ipswich, occupation unknown, noted in his will of 1632 that, 'I have written this my last will and testament with my own hands'. Thomas Gilbert of Orford, Suffolk, a yeoman, bequeathed 10 shillings to Thomas Bond 'for making this will' in 1629. Otherwise, instances of generic phraseology are suggestive of a scribal hand, although not conclusively so.

It is important to reflect that not everybody made a will in seventeenth-century England. Possessing nothing of any great value, the very poor almost never wrote one. Only the wealthier sort had reason to formally set their affairs in order, including well-to-do yeomen, husbandmen, skilled craftsmen, gentlemen, and aristocrats. Women who predeceased their husbands were not by law entitled to make a will: their goods were legally the latter's property. Widows with adequate assets, on the other hand, could draw up a last will and testament if they so wished, for they were no longer bound by the constraints imposed on them by marriage. The widow Marie Holbrooke of Manchester had lots to give away in her will dated 13 November 1660. She bequeathed £100 (approximately £10,500 in 2019), eight pieces of gold, brass and pewter, silver plate, a bedstead, bedding, and her best looking glass to her son Richard alone. Nevertheless, with these considerations in mind, experts in the field have concluded with relative confidence that many more men made wills than women in early modern England.

Like it has always done, and continues to do in the present day, the will held immense power over English society. It could snub the undeserving and reward the worthy with the flourish of a nib. It had the capacity to tear families apart, or bring them closer together. Fortunes might be made and ruin unleashed, all because of a fateful clause. Consequently, the will of Sir Richard Assheton caused heated scenes in Lancashire in 1617. Richard's death was calm enough, but one particular beneficiary was anything but relaxed once the patriarch's last wishes had been read out. His eldest son and namesake, Richard, was so riled by the instructions left by his father (which intimated that his brother should have a share in the family home and its valuables) that he demanded the keys to Middleton Hall there and then. He also insisted that he be given the family plate immediately, which he believed was his by right. When the executors would not yield, Richard fell out with them too. For many, though, the drama surrounding a contested will paled into insignificance when compared to the immediate and unsightly problem left in a person's wake after they had died: the corpse.

Chapter 5

Of Corpses, Coffins, and Carriages

'Let me behold my corpse which lieth folden in searclothes, leaded and coffined here before me yet unburied and consider: he was as I am, and as he is, I shall be. His candle is put out, his fire is quenched and he hath made his bed in the dark.'[1]

Lady Grace Mildmay, noblewoman and expert medical practitioner, was overcome with emotion when confronted with the body of her dead husband, Sir Anthony, in Northamptonshire in 1617. Sir Anthony's death was not in itself unexpected, but for his wife the motionless earthly remains left behind came as something of a painful shock. The sight of his corpse compelled her to meditate on the fragile nature of life and death; she imagined his life as a flame that had now been extinguished, leaving in its wake only a cold and dimmed room. Her husband had 'made his bed in the dark'. Lady Grace considered how Sir Anthony had been here one minute, and was gone the next, the whole process seeming bewilderingly fast, and how eventually she would disappear in the same rapid way. As it happened, she wouldn't have long to wait. Her own death occurred just three years later in 1620.

A dead body could be a difficult sight to come to terms with in seventeenth-century England, particularly in a Protestant country that had, since the English Reformation of the previous century, agreed to abandon the practice of intercessory prayer, a Catholic hangover that involved praying for the dead. Yet even though the cadaver might produce strong emotions from grieving relatives and make day-to-day living difficult to get through, there were practical things that needed to be done. The dead body required attention before it could be buried. Depending on a person's status and the amount of money he or she had, the process could be lengthy and costly, comprising a number of different steps that aimed to get the corpse from the bed to the grave in a manner that was both befitting and subtly pragmatic.

It was sometimes felt necessary to begin with an autopsy if the cause of death of an individual was unclear. Of course, in a period of inferior medical understanding, this lack of clarity was ubiquitous. The Reverend John Ward of Stratford-upon-Avon commented on autopsies frequently in his diary, intermittently performing them himself, and on other occasions watching on with great interest as a surgeon did the work. In around 1659 he saw a Mr Gwinne opened up. Ward related that he 'could perceive nothing in him that might cause his death', and continued:

> 'His spleen was somewhat flaccid, so was his heart, and one of his kidneys; but his lungs had some kind of schirrhus in them, and in those schirrhi, a sabulous kind of matter, but that could not kill him. They pretended hee had a contusion of the liver, in regard that the concavitie of itt was a little stained; but possibly itt was nothing but the settling of the blood when death came.'[2]

In 1666, when Ward assisted in the post-mortem examination of the aforementioned Mrs Townsend of Alverston, the cause of death was much more easy to identify. Her breast was opened on the surface and found to be 'very cancrous' inside. A yellowish substance oozed out of the patient as they inspected the diseased tissue. The flesh that had grown back in the breast after Mrs Townsend's failed operation was of a 'hard gristly' consistency, Ward reported, yet as they cut further into the organ they could locate no further trace of the disease, which confused both men. The vicar recorded that they would have cut further into the tissue had it not been for the fact that they lacked sponges and other necessary equipment to carry out the procedure properly. In a third example, which Ward documented but at which he was not present, a dead child was cut open and found to have died because it could not 'discharge its urine'. A stone was discovered filling up the 'pelvis of the kidney', with a 'sharp point stopping the point of the kidney'.

Aggressive and fast-spreading diseases like plague naturally attracted the interest of surgeons, who appeared eager to apply their knives to victims of the disease. A letter written to the Dean of St Paul's Cathedral, Dr William Sancroft, provides a window on the practice and its associated dangers in 1665:

> 'Dr. Burnett, Dr. Glover, and one or two more of the College of Physicians, with Dr. O'Dowd…some surgeons, apothecaries, and Johnson the chemist, died all very suddenly. Some say…that these, in a consultation together, if not all, yet the greatest part of them, attempted to open a dead corpse which was full of the tokens [orange, black, blue, or purple spots on the skin]; and being in hand with the dissected body, some fell down dead immediately, and others did not outlive the next day at noon.'[3]

The story seems far-fetched and may have been nothing more than hearsay, but there was probably some truth behind it. Dissecting a corpse infected with plague was never going to be a risk-free procedure by its very nature. Although the dissectors almost certainly did not drop down dead where they were standing, it is likely that some of them went away and died later.

Professionals opened up the corpses of hanged criminals throughout the seventeenth century, but not so that autopsies might be conducted on them. Anatomists were given access to felons' cadavers so that they could dissect and study the human body. The practice succeeded in achieving two things at once: the criminal continued to be punished after death by having his or her body dismembered, while from a medical perspective anatomical knowledge was enhanced. The dissection of criminals gained momentum in England only in the middle of the sixteenth century, following staggered royal consent to the procedure by King Henry VIII in 1540 and Queen Elizabeth I in 1565. The former allowed four felons to be cut open annually by the Company of Barbers and Surgeons. One hundred years later, criminal dissection had become firmly established in the country. William Harvey, an early theorist on the circulation of blood around the body, carried out many dissections on deceased delinquents in early seventeenth-century London. By the 1660s, commentators were referring to the act with apparent indifference. The antiquary

Anthony Wood mentioned rather offhandedly in 1663 that several young physicians had travelled from Oxford to Aylesbury to 'dissect a woman that was there executed for felony'.

Anatomical lecture halls became public theatrical spaces overnight, or so it seemed, with the general population having developed an appetite for seeing bloody dissections in the flesh. In February 1663, Samuel Pepys attended one such performance at the Barber-Surgeons' Hall in London. Kidneys and ureters were the chosen topics of the evening. Afterwards, having eaten a delicious dinner, Pepys was invited to a private viewing of the corpse that had landed the starring role in the show, a seaman hanged for larceny. The diarist noted that the body was cold to the touch, and made for an 'unpleasant sight'. The Murder Act of 1752 saw the public dissection of criminals convicted of homicide become mandatory. Until then, however, the sentence was handed out on a case-by-case basis. Most men and women had no need to even consider the possibility of being malevolently dissected by the state after they had died, let alone fret over it. Hanged felons were in the minority, dissected felons more so.

The immediate fate of the majority of corpses in seventeenth-century England depended on the status of the individual in question. Members of the nobility and the very wealthy were often embalmed in the first few hours after death had occurred. This was done to prevent the body from festering while preparations for the funeral, which were usually large affairs and therefore required time to plan, were made. The French surgeon Philibert Guibert described the intricate process of embalming in 1639, beginning with the removal of the organs. He initially advised his readers to make an incision in the cadaver from the neck to the lower belly, which would allow the easy extraction of the heart, lungs, stomach, bowels, bladder, and diaphragm. These were to be deposited in 'a large basin or vessell'. Next, Guibert indicated that the skull should be sawn in half and the brain removed. The brain was to be placed in the aforementioned vessel also, along with the rivers of blood that had flown from the body during its preliminary treatment. Note that it was important to keep the said receptacle, full to bursting with body parts, for later use. It was routinely the case that organs were buried as part of the wider burial rites of the deceased person. Sir Richard Brownlow's bowels, for instance, were interred separately to his body in the church at Enfield following his death there in the late 1630s.

Now that the corpse had been emptied, Guibert told his readers, the real work of embalming could commence. First the inside of the skull was to be cleaned with vinegar and stuffed with vinegar-soaked cotton pieces. When this was finished, the two pieces of the skull were to be sewn back together again. Having drained the remaining dregs of blood from every extremity, the rest of the body was to be cleaned with vinegar and filled with cotton, and anointed with 'Venice Turpentine, dissolved in oyle of Roses or oyle of Spike [oil distilled from lavender]'. Finally, the body was to be 'covered over with Sear-cloth'. References to embalming are prevalent in contemporary descriptions. Lucy Hutchinson noted that her husband's body had been embalmed after his death in 1664 'in order to his funeral', as he had 'thrice ordered'. A decade on, in September 1678, John Evelyn recorded that he had been given the unenviable task of having his dear friend Margaret Godolphin embalmed because her husband was too distraught to see to it himself. Evelyn closed her unseeing eyes and 'dropped a tear' upon her cold cheek before he had the young woman 'wrapped in lead'. Whether due to its unmistakeable whiff of status or the potential whiff of rotting flesh, embalming was clearly regarded as an important procedure among elite circles. Some 26 years earlier in August 1652, Robert Sidney took the brazen decision to postpone the burial of his daughter-in-law at Penshurst in Kent because 'they had omitted at London to putt the body in lead'.

For those ordinary folk who were expected to be buried perhaps a day or two after death had claimed them, the preparation of the corpse was much simpler. A modest shroud sufficed to wrap the body in. These were usually made of Holland cloth or some such other plain material; in most cases ordinary sheets were used from the deceased's domestic supply, although sometimes shrouds were bought new for the occasion, costing no more than a few shillings each. The cost of the printer Cantrell Legge's 'winding sheet' was exactly five shillings in Cambridge in 1625. A splash of colour was opted for in rare instances. John Mellege of Poole specified in his will in around 1632 that his executors should not only bury him 'in the finest Holland', but 'wrap his corps in the best crimson plush that could be got'. The guidelines were tightened considerably in the second half of the century. Acts passed in 1666, 1678, and 1680 forbade the burial of the dead in anything but a woollen shroud. This was done in an effort to encourage the development of the country's woollen trade, receiving mixed reactions from the general population.

16. An engraving of the body of a noblewoman laid out on a bed of black velvet, by Lucas Kilian, c.1579-1637. Although the nationality of the woman is unclear, this is a likely representation of the treatment of some seventeenth-century English aristocrats following death. The noblewoman pictured may well have been embalmed before burial.

The Reverend Philip Henry wrote rather stonily in 1667 that a local man had been buried in a shroud made of woollen cloth 'to satisfy the law'. He remarked that the Act, 'being then new, was generally observ'd, though soon after layd aside'. In the 1690s the French writer François Maximilien Misson gave a detailed description of how the English dead were apparelled in his own time, which is worth quoting in full:

> 'After they have wash'd the Body throughly clean, and shav'd it, if it be a Man, and his Beard be grown during his Sickness, they put it on a Flannel Shirt, which has commonly a Sleeve purfled about the Wrists, and the Slit of the Shirt down the Breast done in the same Manner. When these Ornaments are not of Woollen Lace, they are at least edg'd, and sometimes embroider'd with black Thread. The Shirt shou'd be at least half a Foot longer than the Body, that the Feet of the Deceas'd may be wrapped in it, as in a Bag. When they have thus folded the End of this Shirt close to

the Feet, they tye the Part that is folded down with a Piece of Woollen Thread, as we do our Stockings; so that the End of the Shirt is done into a Kind of Tuft. Upon the Head they put a Cap, which they fasten with a very broad Chin cloth; with Gloves on the Hands, and a Cravat round the Neck, all of Woollen.'[4]

The attitude of the people appeared to be straightforward enough. Nothing too fancy was the order of the day, perhaps unsurprisingly in a Protestant country that placed great value on simplicity and humility, and so a shirt and cap would do just fine for the cadavers.

The job of dressing and covering the corpse seemed to fall to women or the poor as a general rule. The procurement of a coffin was less ritualised. At the turn of the seventeenth century this familiar aspect of modern funerals was considered a luxury by most of the population. It was only in the early years of the 1600s that coffin usage actually began to grow in England, being viewed less as an indulgence of the well-off and more a practical means by which to dispose of the dead. A seventeenth-century testator might specify burial in a coffin in his or her will. Ann Ripps of Nacton, widow, stated unequivocally in her will of 1631 that she wished to be buried in one. In the same year, Anne Smith of Ubbeston, spinster, addressed her desire to be put into a coffin in a more precise way. She bequeathed to Robert Smith wood and boards, two iron wedges, and one 'pair of wool cardes', on the proviso that he make a decent coffin for her at his own expense. Coffins continued to be employed as symbols of social superiority even after their popularity had soared. It was all in the detail. Sir Joseph Hayes of Ubbeston, Suffolk knight, knew exactly what he was doing in 1627 when he requested that five yards of black cloth be laid on his coffin immediately after his death. Not just anybody could afford to have their coffin adorned; the addition of expensive cloth connoted wealth and status from beyond the grave. Subtle touches like this separated the haves from the have-nots and helped to reinforce the hierarchal systems in place in every parish up and down the country.

For well-heeled Suffolk knights such as Joseph Hayes, it was important to have a good-looking coffin at the ready for when you died. The significance of the coffin for most of the rest of England, however, was in its no-nonsense function as the storage place for a decaying human. After bodies had been embalmed or clothed and shrouded, this is where many of them would have ultimately ended up. Getting a body into a coffin could be easier said than done in this period, especially if disease had left it in a bad way. Oliver Heywood remarked on the coffining of the drunkard Jane Thompson with unconcealed disgust in 1664. The stench alone was said to be intolerable. Frankincense was burned in the room where the corpse rested to alleviate the stink, doing very little, and the awful fumes had soon affected every room in the house. The women who were tending to Jane's body feared that it would burst as they made the necessary preparations for her committal. The coffin, a 'huge great' thing, was quickly brought in. Jane was heaved into the box, but her corpse was so enlarged from liver disease that the lid of the coffin would not close properly, forcing those present to bind it shut with cords. Mercifully, the body of Pepys' uncle was successfully put into a coffin on 6 July 1661, yet the problem of an unpleasant odour remained. The coffin stood on 'two joynt-stools in the chimney in the hall', but was relegated to the yard outside and watched by two men when the smell became too much for the family to stomach.

The bodies of the rich and powerful tended to hang around before being committed to the earth. The corpse of the baronet Simonds d'Ewes' father, Paul d'Ewes, was 'encoffined about six weeks above ground' before it was finally laid to rest in 1631. Over this period of time, be it

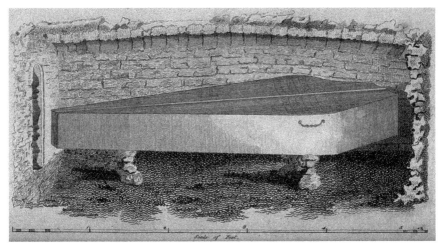

17. An engraving of what a typical seventeenth-century coffin looked like, purported to be that of Charles I's second daughter, Elizabeth. The engraver is unknown.

days or weeks, it was necessary to treat the coffin in a dignified manner that befitted the rank of the person who had died. This might mean setting aside a room especially for the purpose. Sir Charles Lyttelton had the coffin containing the body of Sir Edward Montagu placed in his own private chapel in 1672. The chapel itself was hung with 'black bays' and escutcheons out of respect for the deceased earl, who, as we know, died at sea during the Battle of Solebay. The lying-in-state of the Bishop of Ely five years earlier in 1667 spectacularly surpassed the deference shown to Montagu by the Lytteltons. Matthew Wren had been one of the most authoritative religious figures of the first half of the seventeenth century, and this was to be reflected accordingly in the ostentatious approach to his death. His coffin was brought to Cambridge following his demise on 24 April and positioned in a small room at the University 'darkned and hung in all parts with black cloth'. The corpse was reported to have rested three feet above the floor. Over the coffin was placed a 'black velvett herse cloath' finished with 'white sarcenet'. Only Samuel Newton's descriptions can do justice to the rest of the sumptuous sight:

> 'At the head of the Hearse was standing the Bishops Miter which was either beaten gold or silver guilt, the capp or inpart whereof was crimson sattin or silk, the Miter was plaine saving some little flower wrought on the middle on each side thereof and on the topp of each side a little crosse of about an inch in length and breadth. On the one side of the top of the hearse lay along the Bishopps Crosier of silver somewhat in likeness to a Sheapherds Crooke, of about an ell long, and in thicknes round about 2 inches and a halfe. the floore of the roome was covered either with black cloath or bayes or els was matted; on each side of the herse stood 3 wax tapers in Candlesticks.'[5]

The spectacle did not end there. Two poor scholars in mourning gowns were stationed on either side of the coffin in a display of submission to the dead bishop. The whole performance, for it was a performance, was intended to be seen and experienced by lesser beings. Newton claimed that those who were able to view the body were asked to do so barefooted.

Sometimes people died away from their principal residence in seventeenth-century England. Whereas individuals of limited means were often left to be buried wherever they had perished, the wealthy could afford to be ferried back to their ancestral seats for interment, however far away they may be. Such journeys routinely took place throughout the century; for many, they constituted the natural next step after the cadaver had been embalmed and coffined, being pre-funeral ceremonies in their own right. Family members were expected to follow the hearse as it wound its way out of town and into open countryside, heading for home. Simonds d'Ewes followed the coach carrying the corpse of his father when it departed from the Six Clerks' Office in Chancery Lane in 1631, bound for Stowlangtoft in Suffolk. He continued behind it for a good while, and that night slept 'where the corpse rested'.

Years later in 1678, and with the continued help of John Evelyn, Margaret Godolphin's body was duly sent on its way to Cornwall for burial. Six horses pulled her hearse out of London and southwestwards, their hooves clattering rhythmically against the cobbles as they went. Behind were two additional coaches packed with the courtier's relatives, friends, and servants – around 30 mourners in all. Evelyn went as far as Hounslow with the corpse, but Margaret's husband, still too upset to come to terms with his wife's passing, stayed behind in the capital. During its passage, Godolphin's body was removed from the hearse every night and 'decently placed' wherever the entourage happened to be staying. Decency in this instance entailed surrounding Margaret's coffin with tapers and having her servants watch over her. The corpse's journey to its hometown was not always so grandiose. The remains of the wife of Dr Greene travelled modestly in a hearse from the parish of St Andrews in Cambridge to Linton, Cambridgeshire, in January 1693, she wanting to be buried next to her brother there. In 1665, the body of a Mrs Rosthorne was transported from Bold to Atherton near Manchester in nothing more than a horse litter. The litter was a very basic mode of transport that consisted of a coach strapped to poles, carried between two horses.

Rituals pertaining to the period between death and burial, diligently observed by English men and women for generations, began to be challenged in the 1600s. Social attitudes were partly to blame for this sudden upswing in ceremonial opposition. It has been argued that society was becoming less tolerant towards the sight of dead bodies as it became more cultured and edged towards the Enlightenment of the eighteenth century, meaning that changes in how corpses were prepared for burial were required. However, the major driving force behind the reforms was without question the new religious climate. Long-established Catholic customs were slowly but surely being overruled by Protestant doctrine in England, leading to age-old traditions being snuffed out like candles in a draughty room. One ceremony that seemed to have all but disappeared by 1600 was the tolling of church bells to announce a death. This is what Frederic Gerschow believed as he conducted his tour of England with the Duke of Stettin-Pomerania in 1602 at any rate. Commenting on English habits, he wrote:

> 'They do not ring bells for the dead, but when a person lies in agony, the bells of the parish he belongs to are touched with the clappers until he either dies or recovers again.'[6]

In fact, the practice of ringing church bells to acknowledge a person's death reached far into the century, although its popularity almost certainly diminished as a consequence of the arrival of new religious tastes and ideas. University towns appeared especially keen to keep this ancient institution going. Church bells tolled constantly in Oxford in 1683 during an outbreak of smallpox there, to the extent that officials decided to temporarily ban the exercise because 'many dying frighted people away and caused trading to decay'. Townspeople and traders alike knew exactly what the bells signalled. Ringing for the dead persisted in Oxford's sister town too. Samuel Newton got into the habit of keeping a note of when bells were pealed for this purpose in Cambridge. The 'Esquire Beadle' Thomas Buck, for example, died in the town in 1670; the aforementioned alderman afterwards recorded that, 'the bell rang not for him till next morning'. Once again, the Bishop of Ely easily outdid his contemporaries in terms of the prodigious reception his death received in 1667. On an unassuming Thursday evening Matthew Wren's fresh corpse arrived in Cambridge from London to lie in state in the opulent manner described above. The clamour of church bells was tremendous as the hearse trundled through parish after parish on its slow way to Pembroke College. Newton was fully convinced that every bell along the route pealed for the dead bishop, save for that of St Edward's church, which 'stirred not'.

What, then, did people in this century wear when somebody they knew passed away? Since time immemorial it had been the social duty of those who could afford it to dress in black garments for an extended period of time after the death of a loved one. As much as it was an indication that a family was grieving, it could also be a useful demonstration of status. The observance of mourning represented another custom in the 1600s that was to feel the effects of the sixteenth-century English Reformation. Puritans were less keen on the practice than their forebears had been. Citing Protestant doctrine, they believed mourning clothes were a waste of money that could be better spent on the less fortunate, namely the poor. Such attire was also branded inappropriate, for Protestant standard-bearers were of the opinion that most individuals who wore black didn't truly feel the grief that their sombre dress implied. Mourning was a social statement as opposed to a spiritual one, and this was unacceptable. The gentry's own attitudes towards mourning underwent some changes in this period also, being part of a broader crusade against funeral 'pomp' and 'solemnity', of which more will be spoken later.

We can detect in surviving wills the conflicting views surrounding the wearing of mourning garments in the first half-century of the 1600s. Some testators were for it. The majority of these individuals willed that mourning be given to, or made up for, family members, without specifying when it should be worn or for how long. Suffolk provides a good case study. Sir Thomas Cornwallis of Brome bequeathed in 1604 black cloth to various members of his family, including sisters and nephews, for mourning clothes. Sir Nicholas Bacon of Culford desired in his will of 1624 that his executor, 'give blackes for mourning garments to all my sonnes and sonnes inlawe and daughters and daughters in lawe' after his death. Dame Elizabeth Kitson of Hengrave Hall, knight's widow, specified in her will of 1628 that her executors, 'after my decease…bestowe blacke amonge such as I shall name by my writing subscribed with my owne hand'. Dame Elizabeth made it very clear that it was her choice as to who received blacks, and her choice alone. Servants were common recipients of mourning clothes, as were members of the poor. Sir Thomas Cornwallis in 1604 gave the following instruction:

> 'Item I will that Blacke viz Blacke broade clothe for gownes and Cloakes or Coates shalbe bestowed upon my children and servants and suche of my frendes servants as shalbe [present?] at my funerall'

Along with this request, he willed:

> 'Gownes to five poore menn and five poore women of Wilton
> in Cleveland in Yorkshire And to twoe poore men and twoe
> poore women of...Brome Carley Thrandeston...Palgrave &
> Stuston in the sayde Countie of Suff...to be worne upon the
> daie of my funerall'[7]

Cornwallis desired both his servants and members of the poor to be bedecked in mourning dress after his death, the poor being selected from two counties hundreds of miles apart.

Conversely, several of the Suffolk gentry forbade the wearing of blacks by anybody in their wills, or at the very least attempted to curb the tradition. Edward Bacon of Barham, esquire, willed in 1613 that, 'after my Deathe there be not worne any blacks but by my Wife children and houshold servants'. Dame Anne Drury was even stricter, requesting that no blacks be given after her decease apart from 'to my servants'. One or two testators wholeheartedly prohibited the practice. Sir John Croftes of Little Saxham, knight, instructed in 1627 that he be buried 'without any blacks or mourninge cloathes...because I accompte of

18. A portrait of Katherine Manners in mourning for her husband, George Villiers, 1st Duke of Buckingham, by Henri Beaubrun, c.1628-32. She is dressed mostly in black and carries a portrait miniature of George close to her breast. Mourning came with a strict code in seventeenth-century England, to which the nobility were expected to adhere.

them as Ceremonies that maie well be spared'. So averse to the tradition of mourning garments was Dame Alice Peyton of Great Bradley that she gave to Edmund Davy 40 shillings in money 'instead of' a mourning cloak. She went on to stress that, 'my will is not to have any blackes given' to anybody at all, alluding to the expense of doing so.

Mourning in seventeenth-century England came with a strict code. It continued to be adhered to with rigour throughout the century, even though the ritual itself faced increasing criticism from disapproving onlookers. Lady Isabella Compton, Countess of Northampton, wrote eagerly to her mother, Lady Anne Clifford, to inform her that she had observed mourning in the correct way following the death of Lady Anne's husband, the Earl of Pembroke, in January 1650. Isabella stated that she had put on mourning within four days of the earl's decease, and as per her mother's request, she had not left the house until she was appropriately and respectfully dressed. The mourning wardrobe was extensive and could border on the absurd. In 1686, Edmund Verney sent to his son 'a new black Beavor Hatt', a black 'Crape Hatband', black mourning gloves, black stockings, black shoe buckles, and three pairs of black buttons 'for wrist and neck', along with money for a mourning suit, all as tokens to be worn in the wake of his brother's death. The mourning code went beyond the donning of blacks, however. Hanging rooms with black cloth was considered good practice. If you had the means to cover furniture and riding paraphernalia with black, including saddles and bridles, this was looked upon favourably too. The complexities of the custom caused Edmund Verney Junior to tie himself up in knots in February 1685. He was a young man studying at the University of Oxford at the time, with little knowledge of how things were done there, and King Charles II had just died. Some of his peers took this as a cue to buy mourning. Edmund wrote to his father explaining the dilemma with which he was confronted:

> 'I cannot fully certifie as yet in this matter, But there are two or three fellow Commoners of our House of wch. Mr. Palmer is one, that have bought their Black Cloathes, and Plain Muzeline Bands, and Cloath Shooes, and are now in very strict morning: and others are Preparing for it, so that within this weeke I suppose the greater Part, if not all, of the university will be in morning.'[8]

Edmund Verney Senior wrote back to his son to correct him. He had been in touch with the provost of Oriel College who had clarified that it was usual for one or two people to go into mourning, but no more. Verney ended his response by reminding Edmund Junior, somewhat whimsically, that, 'one swallow or two or three makes no Summer'.

Like everything else, mourning could stray into the realm of high politics in the seventeenth century. The Parliamentarian Colonel Hutchinson was most affronted in 1651 when Oliver Cromwell neglected to send him mourning apparel to observe the passing of the general Henry Ireton. Hutchinson protested that Ireton had been one of his closest friends. He took the gesture, or lack thereof, as a personal brushoff. In an act of defiance, and in stark contrast to the rest of Parliament, Hutchinson turned up at the House of Commons dressed in a scarlet cloak, 'richly laced' and 'such as he usually wore'. The Members were naturally confused. The Parliamentarian explained that Cromwell had chosen not to provide him with an appropriate suit to wear, and therefore he would not 'flatter so much as to buy for himself'. What enraged Hutchinson most of all was that mourning had been bestowed on people who had enjoyed no tangible relationship with Ireton while he was alive. He supposed they had only been kitted out with blacks to make up the train at the funeral. After all, funerals were important affairs.

Chapter 6

The Common and the Noble Funeral

'Now having thus far taken care of the dead body, the next
thing is to consider the reasons and manner of the Pomp
and Ceremony, wherewith the English carry their dead to
the Grave.'[1]

As exemplified in the above remark made by John Dunton in the 1690s,
thoughts inevitably strayed to the funeral in seventeenth-century England
once the corpse had been prepared for burial. There was a strong sense
in this post-Reformation era that funerals were very much for the
living and not the dead. The ceremony was gradually secularised as a
consequence. While all funerals continued to matter, some were more
ostentatious than others. Heraldic funerals were a staple of the gentry
throughout the century, bringing with them lashings of pageantry and
grandiosity, enveloped in a curious sense of ritual. Paupers were more
often than not treated to a simple funeral paid for by the local parish. Be
they big or small affairs, every funerary occasion required some form of
pre-planning. The heralds were charged with the organisation of heraldic
funerals, as the name suggests. They made up a corporation known as
the College of Arms, whose headquarters were based in the City of
London. The College was founded by royal charter in 1484 by King
Richard III, being the culmination of a prolonged era in which heralds
primarily functioned as proclaimers and organisers of tournaments.
In this they acquired an unrivalled knowledge of coats of arms, soon
becoming responsible for controlling their employment. If called upon,

it was the College's job to assemble the forest of banners and escutcheons that befitted a genteel funeral, and to traverse the country to wherever a grand ceremony was being held. No less than three heralds of arms journeyed down to Tawstock, Devon, in May 1605 for the funeral of Elizabeth Bourchier, Countess of Bath. Humbler individuals might rely on the help of kin to plan the funeral of a loved one. After his mother's death in 1693, Robert Meeke, vicar of Slaithwaite in Yorkshire, sought the counsel of his friends to determine what should be done about her funeral. He was clearly distressed by his mother's passing and in need of kindly assistance, much like the husband of Margaret Godolphin had been in 1678. They were happy to oblige.

Most funerals began with a procession to the church. The body of the deceased could be carried in a variety of ways, dependent as always on status and wealth, ranging from resting atop a simple bier to being drawn in a mourning hearse to the church doors. The freedom surrounding this initial ceremony stemmed from contemporary agreement that religion played no part in the transportation of the corpse from its place of preparation to its burial spot. Biers were used to carry the dead in the vast majority of cases, with most churches having at least one at their disposal for the benefit of the whole parish. The bier was a flat wooden structure designed to sit on the shoulders of bearers or on top of a cart or carriage. When carried, this would frequently be performed by family or friends, a commemoration of the intimate relationships that the deceased had enjoyed in life. Nicholas Assheton carried the corpse of his cousin's wife to church in 1617, along with her husband, father, and another cousin called Gyles Parker.

Some seventeenth-century testators wished to have a say on how their corpse got to church on the day of their funeral. The bier was normally alluded to when this occurred, although testators appeared more preoccupied with how many people were to bear their body on its final journey, not who. We return to Suffolk for examples. Elizabeth Gostling of Wilby, widow, asked for four 'young men' to carry her to her grave in 1627, each of whom were to be given gloves worth 12 pence apiece. Yeoman Edward Brame's will of 1628 gave similar instructions, requesting that, '4 several men…bear me to my burial' and be paid 12 pence apiece for their services. John Bateman of Peasenhall, singleman, desired in 1630 that no less than 12 men carry him to Badingham church on his burial day, with the stipulation that the men were to be appointed by the testator himself. James Collin of Little Glemham, singleman, willed in 1627 that,

'Edmund Rowe, Nicholas Fleet, Thomas Ducket, and Thomas Green' be paid five shillings each to bear his body 'to the earth'.

Where a covered coffin was employed, participants might be included to hold up the pall. The Essex craftsman Joseph Bufton painted quite the picture when he noted the funeral procession of the wife of a Mr Boys in November 1685, whose pall was held aloft by six gentlewomen wearing white hoods and nightgowns. Such an extravagant, and somewhat atmospheric it must be said, display was part of the wider processional lavishness at funerals exercised by members of the English nobility across the century. This is where mourning hearses and the like props came to the fore. The gilded funeral of Sir Richard Pigott began in style in 1685 with a procession consisting of two new mourning coaches and a state-of-the-art hearse bearing his black-swathed coffin. Sir Ralph Verney held up the pall as Pigott's coffin entered the church at Quainton in Buckinghamshire. For his service he was given a ring, scarf, hatband, and gloves 'of the best fashion' to wear on the day. 'I had forgotten to tell you that there were abundance of Escutcheons & all Sir Richard's servants were in mourning', he wrote with apparent excitement and wonder to a correspondent later.

The funeral procession of Dorothy Mason, Lady Brownlow, was so exceptional in January 1700 that it was featured in an edition of the *London Post* that month. It was a veritable feast for the eyes, being a passionate response from a grieving widower to the premature death of his wife. First to process from Lady Brownlow's house at Piccadilly towards the location of her funeral at nearby Sutton were two beadles holding black staves and dressed in white scarves. Then came six gentlemen on horseback clad in mourning attire, their 'Cloaks training all over the hinder parts of their Horses'. Following these men was another figure garbed in mourning black, exhibiting a streamer and encircled by a number of attendants carrying unlighted tapers of white wax. More gentlemen marched along the street next, with two more beadles close behind bearing black staves and wearing white scarves, and then 16 more gentlemen on horseback in mourning cloaks, who were themselves accompanied by 16 additional mourners robed in black. A sombre-looking gentleman appeared after that clutching a white rod, silently announcing the approach of Lady Brownlow's hearse. The show continued:

'After him Rode a Minister, followed by the Hearse itself, drawn by 6 Milk White Horses in black Harness, bedeckt with lofty Plumes of Feathers; the Hearse itself was in deep Mourning, beset with rich and deep Escutcheons; the Top of which being elevated with so many Plumes of white Feathers that it seemed a moving Pyramid of Snow. Afterwards came 2 Coaches of State drawn by 6 Horses each, all in Mourning, with mourning Attendants on each side bare-headed. Then followed 4 Coaches, each drawn by 6 Horses, in which were 6 Ladies most solemnly cloathed in deep Mourning, and wrap'd up in White Sarsnet from Head to Foot. [...] All the Coachmen and Postillions had white Gloves, etc., the whole being a most Noble, Glorious, and Costly Cavalcade, the Balconies, Turrets, and Streets of this City being crowded with Spectators to see the same.'[2]

It is hard to imagine such an impressive and melancholic display easing its way through the congested avenues of London. The presence of white amongst the black was not an unfamiliar feature of seventeenth-century English funerals. White as a mourning colour was usually associated with unmarried men and women. Thus, on 20 January 1660, Samuel Pepys recorded that he had been to Westminster Hall and there seen a group of maids wearing white scarves, all of whom had just attended the burial of a young bookseller.

We will meet the poor a little later, but it should be noted here that it was common to see them participating in funeral processions to church. Alice Scrivenor of Ipswich, gentleman's wife, willed right at the beginning of the period in 1600 that, 'black clothe...[be] provided to be bestowed upon twelve poore weomen to be apointed to goe to churche with my bodye at my funerall'. In this case, the 'poore weomen' would most likely be expected to accompany Scrivenor's body to church, not to physically carry the corpse. Sir Thomas Cornwallis, a Suffolk man, recruited poor participants for his funeral from as far away as Cleveland in Yorkshire in 1604. The London widow, Dame Anne Allot, was interested in quantity in 1615 when she willed with precision that at least 40 of the poor women who accompanied her to the grave were 'of the Countie where I nowe dwell at the Discretion of my executor'. Three years earlier Sir Thomas Cambell was similarly preoccupied. At least 76 poor men were to participate in his funeral in the parish of Southwark St Olave in 1612:

19. The vast funeral procession of George Monck, 1st Duke of Albemarle, in 1670. The drawing was made in 1852. His was a typical aristocratic funeral of the seventeenth century, aiming to be respectful, solemn, and impressive all at once. Monck had played a key role in the Restoration of the monarchy and was treated to a burial in Westminster Abbey.

> 'I will that Three score and sixteene gownes be made of some good Cloathe of the price of Seaven shillinges the yard or thereabouts to be given unto three score and sixteene poore men to were them the daye of my funerall whereof all the poore men in the Alley next my house and some other poore men of the parishe and warde and my waterbearer to be one, and ten or twelve of the poorest Ironmongers and the Rest to be suche poore men as my Executors shall appoynte.'[3]

His instructions were seen as kindness to the poor men of his parish, and also an honour. They had been chosen to attend a very grand and wealthy man to his final resting place, to mourn for him as he embarked on the last ritual of his earthly life, which was no small thing.

The streets needed to be clean, tidy, and safe for a substantial funeral procession to journey through. This constituted both a mark

20. An etching of an eighteenth-century funeral procession entering a church by T. Cook, based on a work by William Hogarth. The parish clerk heads the procession, followed by clergymen, the elaborately covered coffin, and mourners walking in pairs. Funeral scenes in the seventeenth century would have been similar in nature to those seen here.

of respect for the deceased individual and a genuine undertaking to remove hazardous waste and obstacles from the ceremonial route. Following the death of Robert Devereux, Earl of Essex, in 1646, an order was issued to the stewards and constables of Westminster to 'pave and cleanse' the streets from Temple Bar to Westminster Abbey, so that everybody taking part in Devereux's procession 'might pass the streets without inconvenience, by reason of the foulness of the ways'. Sometimes streets did not apply to a funeral procession at all – not for most of it, at least. In 1632, before the burial of Mrs Dorothy Lawson, it was the waterways that required clearing around Newcastle most pressingly, not the pavements. She was to be taken to her final resting place in the medieval church of All Saints' in her own boat, as organised by her doting son. On the evening of the funeral her corpse was accordingly carried across the water to Newcastle accompanied by at least 20 other boats and barges. Horses lined the shores. Upon the entourage's arrival on dry land the streets were found to be alight with tapers, being so bright that it seemed more like midday than nighttime. Magistrates, aldermen, and large crowds were waiting at the docking place for Mrs Lawson's coffin, which was draped in a black velvet cloth adorned with a white satin cross. It was then carried to the church to be buried.

The procession now over, it was time to proceed through the heavy church doors, or for some to gather at a particular spot in the churchyard. The greater part of the English population would expect to have a sermon preached at this point, but not everybody was afforded such a luxury. The funeral sermon itself, predictably, came under fire in the seventeenth century from disapproving Protestants, who believed with a certain amount of revulsion that it had morphed into a successor to the Catholic intercessory mass. On a parish level, the feel of a sermon and much of its basic content probably changed very little from the Jacobean to Restoration eras. Overriding concerns, as observed in surviving wills, were the precise passage from the Bible to be preached and the identity of the preacher conducting the service, although written instructions were all too often vague, giving only the bare minimum of information for an executor to act on. The widow Margaret Wolverston desired in her will of 1626 that a nameless 'good preacher' be paid 10 shillings to preach on an unnamed topic at her funeral in Suffolk. In contrast, the yeoman Hugh Butcher of Wilby specified six years earlier in 1620 that a sermon be preached at his funeral 'to the edification and instruction of such persons present'. Right at the beginning of our period, in 1601, Alexander Eylmer of Woodbridge, sailor, mimicked these words with the instruction:

> '…at the day of my funerall when the people shall be, or are gathered togeather, that some learned man shall make unto them a sermon, to the edifieinge of those that shall be there.'[4]

Because both wishes were so syntactically similar, one wonders if the phraseology was a generic construction employed by scribes of the period.

In some instances, well-versed testators singled out a particular excerpt from the Bible that they wished to be included in their funeral sermon, possibly as a means of guaranteeing a level of control over proceedings. Spinster Katherine Jessop of Weybread willed in 1630 that a sermon be preached at her funeral based on the fourth chapter of St Paul's epistle to Timothy (2 Timothy 4), commencing from the line, 'I have fought a good fight'. The Christianly theme of 'fighting the good fight' and faithfully serving God in the face of trials was a popular one at early modern funerals. It was occasionally requested that a testator's initial sermon be the first in a commemorative series. This casts light on the nuanced relationship between funerary wishes and seventeenth-century ideas of posthumous remembrance. The will of yeoman John Felgate of Stonham Aspall is a case in point. In 1623 he instructed his executrix to procure eight sermons to be preached at Stonham Aspall church, Suffolk, namely one at his burial, one a year later, and 'so successively for six more years'. Stipulations of this nature were perhaps symptomatic of the post-Reformation yearning to make certain the enduring remembrance of an individual in the wake of death's oblivion.

The identity of the preacher occupied the minds of those who hankered for a send-off that reminded the congregation of the close ties of kinship that the testator had been blessed with in life. Robert Basse of Ipswich, yeoman, 'humbly desired' in 1626 that his 'friend', the Reverend Samuel Ward, preach a sermon at his funeral. Robert Knapp of Needham Market, yeoman, likewise bequeathed 20 shillings to his friend Mr Fletcher for a funeral sermon. Dame Alice Peyton willed in 1626 that her nephew Adrian 'preach at my funerall if he can'. The presence of the local rector at the funeral of a parishioner publicly demonstrated and reinforced the deceased's clear-cut association with the parish in which they had lived, and so was likewise a popular request. Its attractiveness is strikingly demonstrated in the will of Thomas Armond. Although a parishioner of Rendlesham, Suffolk, he wished to be buried in Bucklesham churchyard around 12 miles away in 1634; yet it was still the parson of Rendlesham whom he entreated to preach a sermon at his funeral, 'if the minister of Bucklesham will allow him to do so'. The desire was mirrored on the opposite side of the country, at the opposite end of the century. The widow Juliana Popham of Thurloxton, Somerset, included a clause in her will setting aside 10 shillings for the minister of Thurloxton, Timothy Lockett, for the delivery of a sermon at her funeral in the 1660s. Most ministers were only too pleased to perform at the funerals of their dead parishioners. From a religious perspective they were duty-bound to do so, but there had to be a degree of willingness from them as well. It would have been a mistake to assume that a minister would agree to preach at every funeral offered to him. The vicar Henry Newcome ran hot and cold in his feelings towards delivering funeral sermons. At times he was content to preach, as on 5 December 1657, when Newcome revealed no outward displeasure at having to orate at the funeral of one Francis Hollinworth, the father of his religious predecessor. On other occasions, however, the vicar appeared most irritated by his godly obligations in respect of laying the dead to rest. The following year, in May 1658, Newcome wrote that he had been 'forced out' on the Sabbath to preach at the funeral of 'old Mrs Hartley'. He was ill with a cold at the time and found performing difficult.

Funeral sermons themselves became a recognised means of paying tribute to the deceased, as well as expounding the Bible to the congregation, with the advent of the printed sermon at the turn of the seventeenth century ensuring that these personalised texts would act as remembrances for many years after a person's death. The sermon delivered at the funeral of Lady Margaret Mainard of Little Easton, Essex, printed in 1682, listed many of her best qualities:

> 'As a Mother she was unspeakably tender, and carefull, of the two Children [...] Her near Relations, and all that were blest with her friendship, had a daily share in her intercessions, all their concerns, all their afflictions were really her own; her chief kindness was for their Souls, and she lov'd them with a charity...'[5]

These stirring words could now be forever retained through ink and paper.

Seventeenth-century funerals did not always go according to plan. Mishaps were more common than one might expect, ranging from the trivial to the serious. The antiquary Anthony Wood recorded with amusement that strong winds had blown a sexton's hat off in 1675 while he had been grave-digging in the church of St Dunstan-in-the-West in Fleet Street, during the funeral of Richard Sanders. The scenes at York Minster in 1686 were less comical. On the day of Lady Henrietta Strafford's funeral a riot erupted in the streets between townsmen and soldiers. Beginning with the 'rabble', as described by Sir John Reresby, targeting Lady Strafford's decorated hearse as it approached the Minster and tearing the escutcheons from it, the ruckus soon spilled into the cathedral as resisting troops were pushed back by the assaulting force of local men. Black cloth that had been hung with care around the Minster's choir was pulled down and stolen, and several on each side were hurt. Ineffective crowd control was without doubt the main cause of funerary disruption in England in the 1600s. Henry Newcome estimated that an astonishing 4,000 poor persons turned up at the funeral of Mrs Moseley in Lancashire in 1662, resulting in a child being killed in the crowd and one John Broxup falling from his horse and badly hurting himself. The throngs were worse at the funeral of Lady Ramsey, widow of Sir Thomas Ramsey, Lord Mayor of London, in November 1601. The number of beggars who descended on Leadenhall Market to benefit from the funeral dole was said to be so 'excessive and unreasonable' that 17 people were trampled to death in the ensuing scrum.

That said, it was accepted and even anticipated that the poor would show up at such distinguished events, although probably not by the thousands. The handing out of a dole to the poor was an important part of the seventeenth-century English funeral, deriving from the medieval custom of posthumous almsgiving. One could continue to be the charitable Christian even after death by providing for the less fortunate at one's burial. It was a form of early modern parish poor relief in all but name, continuing to be implemented at a steady pace until 1700 and beyond. Lured by the potential gains in doing so, testators often provided for a funeral dole in their wills. Doles could range from a modest offering of two pennies per poor person to the more considerable sum of £10 or more, the latter intended to be divided between every needy soul present on the day. The amount a testator set aside for a funeral dole clearly depended on their wealth and rank. Whereas Thomas Watson, a fisherman from Aldeburgh, merely willed that two pennies be handed out to every poor person in attendance at his funeral, William Buckenham of Yoxford, styled 'gentleman' in his will of 1632, desired that a more substantial £5 be distributed amongst the poor of the parish 'at my burial'. The point is illustrated more vigorously still when considering the amounts the gentry earmarked for doles. Sir Thomas Cornwallis of Brome, knight, ordered his executor to bequeath to the poor at his funeral the large sum of £20 in 1604. Aside from constituting charitable gestures commensurate with the prosperity of such men, considerable sums like these may have been used to attract as sizeable a funeral crowd as possible. Large numbers at a seventeenth-century funeral could be interpreted as a gesture of respect for the deceased person. A good turnout was a way of symbolically reinforcing the regard that men such as Cornwallis had been shown (or felt that they had been shown) in life as prominent, influential, and high-ranking members of the local community. A sense of parish identity was upheld from beyond the grave, and more specifically the hierarchical relationship between parish and parish elite was preserved.

Some doles came in the form of bread. At the turn of the seventeenth century it was common enough for this foodstuff to be given to the poor at large funerals in London in place of pennies. The practice was still going in Suffolk in the 1620s. Margaret Taseburgh of Ipswich, widow, desired in 1623 that her executor distribute 20 dozen loaves of bread 'amongst such poor as he think fit' at her funeral. Edward Wallys, an ironmonger of Ipswich, willed two years later that 10 shillings be given out in bread to the poor of three parishes 'at his funeral, or soon after'. Yeoman Robert Aldhouse of Fressingfield went further, requesting that the poor of Fressingfield 'that shall come to the funeral…[shall] have in competent manner bread, cheese & beer at the said time, for their relief'. The trio of testators may have anticipated that the poor were more likely to be tempted into attendance with the immediate promise of food, as opposed to money. Perhaps they were too deprived themselves to afford a monetary dole.

On the flip side of the coin, some in seventeenth-century England seemed to have no time for the custom whatsoever. It was not unknown for a testator to actively forbid the distribution of doles at their funerals. Testator Robert Hawes of Brandeston, yeoman, made plain in his will of 1624 that, 'there shall be no concourse of poor people at [his] funeral [and] no dole to be then given'. John Cornwallis of Earl Soham, esquire, emphasised his personal aversion to funeral doles in 1615 through the assertive use of the first person: '*my will* is that there shoulde bee noe concourse of poore people at my burial and that noe dole bee then given'. Taking into consideration the calamitous events that unfolded at the funerals of both Lady Ramsey in 1601 and Mrs Moseley in 1662, this kind of hardnosed attitude is unsurprising. The banning of funeral doles has been understood in hindsight as an attempt on the part of the noble and rich to prevent disorderly mobs from spoiling a polished and dignified occasion. When funeral doles *were* given the green light, there were complaints that they had been ungratefully received in any case. The Reverend Philip Henry expressed his views in a forthright manner following the burial of his Aunt Adams in Malpas, Cheshire, in the 1660s:

> 'Aunt Adams was buried according to her desire in her will, at Malpas. Mr. Bridge preach't – twas the first buryal of which I was supervisor, and I was forc't in some things to submit to custom, tho' against my own inclination. Concerning dole I gave groats apiece to about 20 poor of this parish, and at Malpas gave 20s. to poor there at pence apiece & yet they were not satisfied: many from neighb. parishes went away from the house clamouring which I was troubled at.'[6]

The vicar seemed a dour sort, no doubt spurred on by a deep sense of spiritual indignation. On the morning of the funeral, Henry wrote that, 'I rather permitted than desired' the ringing of the church bells at Worthenbury near Wrexham.

With the funeral drawing to a close, it was at last time to offer up the body to the earth. In exceptional circumstances the corpse was buried days before the main event had occurred. The Countess of Bath was interred at Tawstock on the day she died in March 1605, yet her funeral did not take place until some weeks later on 6 May. For most, however, burial came last in seventeenth-century England, where it belonged. To be at the graveside and staring down into the dark abyss, both metaphorically and literally, was an emotional moment for family and friends. Particularly upsetting were the burials of small children. Ralph Josselin's little boy was buried 'with the teares and sorrow' of his parents and many neighbours in February 1648. Two doctors' widows agreed to place the baby in his grave, which Ralph believed to be 'not onely a testimonie of their love to mee, but of their respect to my babe'. Just two years after losing his son, Josselin found himself bidding farewell to his daughter's body too. Mary was buried in Earls Colne church on 28 May 1650. Two widows and Josselin's sister carried the eight-year-old girl to her grave, while Ralph took it upon himself to lower the corpse into the earth, having first kissed his daughter goodbye on the lips. In this moment history had repeated itself. After the northerner Nicholas Assheton's baby died in 1618, whom we first encountered right at the beginning of this book, the poor little thing was also laid in its grave with the touching assistance of its father, as well as its grandmother.

It was usually the job of the sexton to dig the grave. He was a paid parish official with menial responsibilities in and about the local church. Samuel Pepys met with a gravedigger in London in 1664 and was horrified by the man's crude proposal in respect of his brother's burial. Speaking about the rotting corpses already entombed underneath St Bride's church, the sexton assured him, 'I will justle them together but I will make room for him'. One can imagine Pepys' wig jumping at the very thought of it. Through sheer overcrowding alone, particularly in the capital, the sexton couldn't dig a hole wherever he fancied in the 1600s. But there were other considerations to be made. The highest stratums of society expected a church burial, ideally in the chancel. This was a legacy of the medieval period, when patrons (often noteworthy figures) sought burial close to where they had sat in church. By the seventeenth century, to be buried inside a church was viewed as a privilege that only people of a certain ilk could obtain. It was costlier for one thing, but interior interment had also acquired a social prestige that caused it to be quite beyond the reach of those who were deemed unworthy of the honour, which happened to be most of the population. The aristocracy and those with money to burn were prime candidates for church burial, and they knew it. Sir Humphrey Handford, alderman of the City of London, asked to be buried in the church of St Mary Woolchurch Haw in a vault he had already prepared for himself in 1625. There was no question of his not getting what he wanted. Sir Francis Nedham thought being buried in Barking church was acceptable in his will of 1637, but even better in his eyes would be interment in the chapel of the 'College or Schoole' he was building at the time. For everybody else, comprising humble tradesmen, those in service, and the poor, burial in the local parish churchyard would have to do. The churchyard was less sacred than the church, but it was consecrated ground nonetheless.

The sexton, perhaps paid a few shillings for his work, similarly needed to think about whom the deceased person wanted to be buried near or next to when carrying out his assignment. It is popularly believed that familial relationships were lukewarm in seventeenth-century England; the early modern family is thought to have been based on a strict patriarchal system in which members came and went rapidly on account of high rates of mortality, leaving little room for affection. That so many relatives chose to lie together in death suggests otherwise. On a purely factual level, families had been buried together for centuries so that everybody could be found in one particular area of a church or churchyard. Yet there is an argument to be put forwards that the changeable religious climate of the seventeenth century, and the resulting uncertainty of what happened to you after you died, provoked many into choosing to be by their loved ones' side after death, as a form of comfort perhaps. People wanted to stay together. Genuine affection must have played a part. Seventeenth-century testators often asked to be buried by their husbands or wives, or parents, or children even. In the 1620s Dame Alice Peyton of Great Bradley asked to be buried 'in the same place and vault where the corps of my deare husband lye interred'. Widow Margery Page, on the other hand, chose to lie in Blakenham churchyard on the hill 'where my mother and father were buried'. The Earl of Leicester summed up the sentiment of these arrangements nicely in October 1651 when he remarked that his daughter had been buried, 'as she desyred, betweene or very near her two sisters, Mary and Elizabeth, who, I hope, are all together in heaven'. Parish burial registers reveal that in the event that multiple family members perished at the same time, bodies might even share the same coffin. In the London parish of St Michael, Cornhill, in 1625, Mrs Ellinor Hussey, who had presumably died in childbirth, was buried in a coffin with her baby. A third of a century later, in 1660, two children of a Mr Thomas Simpson were committed to the earth in the same coffin in York.

The burial was not quite the end of the story. Feasts, dinners, and 'drinkings' habitually occurred after the dead had been put to rest. Such revelries helped bring a parish together and strengthened social and especially neighbourly relations following tragedy, being even more important towards the end of the century when funeral customs had lost much of their essential religious worth. They might also act as a means of displaying the affluence of the late individual. Sometimes food was provided before the ceremony, as in the case of the funeral of Samuel Pepys' brother in 1664. On this occasion wine and burnt claret were served to guests in the house before the corpse was taken to church. Mourners were treated to an all-out banquet before the body of Dorothy Lawson was carried across the water to Newcastle in 1632 for interment. More conventionally, attendees at the funeral of Tom Starkie's wife in Lancashire in 1617 were invited to a dinner at Middleton Hall after the service had concluded, where meat was served aplenty. Roger Lowe of Ashton-in-Makerfield fasted before the funeral of Ann Taylor in 1666, expecting 'according to custome' to be provided with refreshments once her body had been committed to the earth.

He was sorely disappointed when, sat ready at a table with his neighbours, the vicar approached the waiting party and stated that no drinks were to be filled until prayers had been said. Luckily for Roger, his friend Thomas Harison supplied him with a cup and a half of 'good pottage' on their return home, and thus catastrophe was avoided. Provision for a post-funeral spread was occasionally made in wills. In 1612 Sir Thomas Cambell gave the Ironmongers' Company £20 'to make them a Dynner uppon the Daye of my buryall, unto the which Dynner I will have invited all the widdowes and wyves of all suche whose husbandes have ben wardens'.

Pious bystanders continued to worry about the custom of funeral feasting as late as the 1690s. In 1692, the Reverend Robert Meeke wrote fearfully:

> 'Had a funeral at Slaithwaite – had the drinking at Crimble. We have a very ill custom at funerals – turning mourning into drinking, feasting, and mirth – Lord, heal, reform, forgive the disorders and sins amongst us.'[7]

As far as Meeke was concerned, funerals were not a time for senseless merry-making. Oliver Heywood, the Yorkshire minister, agreed with his clerical peer. Sinful drinking after burials went down especially badly with the clergy, but even those upstanding members of the Christian community such as Heywood himself could be tempted into the practice from time to time. An episode in 1676 saw the minister keeping company with a group of drinkers in a tavern following the funeral of 'old Rich'. Things were made considerably worse by the fact that the official funeral drinking had already finished. Heywood observed in his diary:

> '...after the drinking at Stump-cross, a company of fellows would needs drink 2d a peece, I sate down with them, and though I did not drink, yet I did not appear so much as I ought agt their vain way of drinking shots, I saw some lay at it busily, and strove to drink, I left them at it, and am afraid many of them will get too much – I am conscious to myself I was not so faithfull to my god as I ought, though I did say something to dissuade them from intemperance.'[8]

Oliver was able to resist the bottle. His regret came in having not attempted to persuade the rest of the revellers to put down their own.

The man could be proud at least that he had not followed the example of his fellow preacher Dr Hook, who, it was whispered, often got so drunk before sermons that he could neither preach nor 'read prayers sensibly'.

Probate accounts show that refreshments were an expensive part of seventeenth-century funerals. In many instances they were *the* most expensive part. The charges for the burial of Joseph Bufton's grandmother in 1658 are put into context in her probate accounts:

For wine	£1 10s
For sugar	3s 4d
For gloves	5s 2d
For 24 gallonds of beer	8s 4d
For a coffin	6s
For ye burial	2s 4d[9]

Wine was the most expensive addition to her funeral, costing over £1, followed by the 24 gallons of beer that were offered to guests on the day, which came to over eight shillings. The coffin was only six shillings. Funerals in England were pricey in general in the 1600s, which is why the poorest could not afford them. Costs for various items only grew dearer as the century progressed. By the time Bufton was putting together the accounts for his father's burial in 1695, the local cost of a coffin had risen to £1, 27 gallons of beer set you back 17 shillings, a funeral sermon was worth another £1, and four 'gallons of sack' came to £1 and 12 shillings. Robert Meeke was aghast at the cost of his mother's funeral in 1693, which in all totalled a massive £60. 'Following worldly customs maketh many needless expences at such times', he wrote on reflection, probably with a sigh. The funerals of the great and good amounted to daylight robbery. The Bishop of Winchester, James Montague's, funeral cost a whopping £940 to put on in 1618 (approximately £124,000 in 2019), even after he had expressly instructed in his will that expenses should not exceed £400.

The time of day at which a funeral was held carried significance in seventeenth-century England. Heraldic funerals of the elite tended to take place in daylight hours, but increasingly nighttime burials were preferred by members of the English nobility. There may have been a few reasons why the aristocracy chose to rebel in this way, indicative of the broader changes seen in funerals from approximately 1600 onwards.

A new crusade against pomp and solemnity, stemming from Protestant values, meant that the landed gentry and others were ever more inclined to plump for modest burials reflective of the national faith. Modesty was achieved best in the dead of night, when the rest of the world slept. Active distaste for the heraldic funeral was another key motive. Such ceremonies were predominantly concerned with the ritualistic replacement of the noble dead with their aristocratic successors, favouring formality over familiarity. They were also expensive and complex to organise. Nocturnal funerals slipped through the heralds' net unnoticed and allowed for a more personalised and simpler goodbye. Mourners intimately attached to the deceased person could be chosen to attend the corpse in place of officials who were obliged to be present; family could likewise gather and grieve in peace within the quietness and closeness of a darkened church. Nighttime burials in themselves were sombre, private affairs, where one could appreciate the loss of a life away from the ceremonial preoccupations of the heraldic funeral.

Funerals in the night crop up with relative frequency in contemporary records, demonstrating their mounting popularity. Samuel Newton reported that William Alington of Horseheath Hall was buried on a Tuesday night in February 1685. According to the scrupulous weaver Joseph Bufton, Sir Mark Guyon, knight, who died in the 1690s, was buried at night in Coggeshall at the church of St Peter ad Vincula in the following manner:

> '…was buried about 10 o'clock in ye evening, by torches, without a sermon; there was about 30 or 40 men had black gowns and caps yt carried ye torches to light ye coaches; there was one wreath of black cloth hung round ye chancill, and ye pulpit was covered with black and ye great Bible.'[10]

For a knight, the above was quite an understated affair. The nobility made sure to mention nighttime funerals in their wills. Dame Elizabeth Kitson of Hengrave Hall made a direct link in 1628 between lack of pomp and burial in the hours of darkness. She desired that there was to be no solemnity at her funeral, and therefore willed to be buried 'earlie in the morning, or late in an Eveninge', with only her friends and servants in attendance.

Not everybody took to the development. Some considered nocturnal funerals to be an insult to the memory of highborn men and women.

Commenting on the funeral of Sir Thomas Barnardiston at Kedington in 1619, Simonds d'Ewes complained:

> '[It] was in the night, without any manner of solemnity befitting the antiquity of his extraction, or the greatness of his estate.'[11]

Similar hostility surfaced in August 1652. The Earl of Salisbury was irate when he learned that his daughter Lady Catherine had been interred in the night at the Sidneys' family church in Kent, in a private fashion and 'without any ceremony'. Robert Sidney, Lady Catherine's father-in-law, made the brisk rebuttal that Salisbury's eldest daughter had been buried in the same way, even though she had been married to a man who practically outranked Catherine's husband, in 'the times, which then were much fitter for expence and solemnity then these are now'. Plans to rid a daytime funeral of pomp and solemnity could also be hotly contested. Sir Ralph Verney's will caused quite the stir when it was opened following his death in 1696. The family could not understand what the old man was getting at when he wrote that he wished to be buried 'as privately and with as little pomp as may be'. Surely it was a slip of the quill pen. A relation, Peg Adams, aired the household's confusion when she reasoned in a letter:

> 'I should have thought that a man so generally known to be loved in the country, it would have been very decent to have some of the gentry carry him to his grave.'[12]

In the end it was decided to respect Ralph's wishes. His funeral might as well have taken place at night. When the day came, the pouring rain made everything so dark in Middle Claydon that those travelling back from the church in carriages did not dare to pull the windows up, for reasons that remain a little unclear.

The heraldic funeral survived the seventeenth century, but it had been undermined by a fluctuating and divided nation. With the heralds' decline in influence came the slow rise of the undertaking profession in the last few decades of the 1600s. Cutting costs while maintaining an impression of decency became a priority of funerals in Restoration England. Craftsmen reacted to the national appetite by advocating the cheaper alternative of renting out funeral furnishings, as opposed to selling them. The funeral trade was consequently reinvented as the booming commercial enterprise recognisable today, with the aforementioned artisans becoming the country's first undertakers. One of the byproducts of the movement was the introduction of funeral invitation tickets, which helped to propagate the idea of burials as full-blown advertised events. The invitation ticket, put together by undertakers, was often elaborately decorated and aimed to persuade the recipient through novel eccentricity to come along to the funeral. It probably worked. The commerciality of funerals was further amplified by the appearance of undertakers' advertisements in broadsheets and on trade cards, which listed meticulously the services and goods that such tradesmen had to offer.

Thus, strong and difficult to avoid was the tide of commercialisation by 1700. Funerals had evolved a great deal over the preceding 100 years in England. At the same time, and in an ageless manner, they had changed very little in terms of their basic components. Occasions that did more or less manage to retain their core form throughout the century were the funerals of royalty.

Chapter 7

Royal Funerals

Royal funerals were like no other ceremonial event in seventeenth-century England. They were staged with much more in mind than the simple laying to rest of the deceased sovereign. In one sense, they functioned as displays of power and pomp in the wake of a monarch's death, visually representing the authority of the monarchy in the grey space between the demise of one royal ruler and the formal accession of the next. But these majestic and dignified occasions were also performed for other reasons: to introduce the emergent figure of the new sovereign, for instance, and to showcase and reinforce social hierarchies through grand funeral processions. Royal funerals were without question designed to dazzle the senses, while at the same time sobering the heart and evoking in a curiously profound way the mournful emotion of melancholy. As continues to be the case today, the funeral of a monarch constituted an important last ritual in the lifecycle of their reign, particularly if it had been a long and prosperous one. It provided an opportunity for people of all ranks, from all backgrounds, to pay their final respects, and to reconcile with the sombre reality that their most high and mighty leader was no more.

Seventeenth-century England witnessed its first royal funeral on 28 April 1603, following the much lamented death of Queen Elizabeth I around two months earlier on 24 March. A surviving relic of her own Golden Age and the wider Tudor faction established by her grandfather, Henry VII, Elizabeth's death was an especially poignant event because it was viewed by many as the end of an era. As well as being the last of the Tudor monarchs, Elizabeth was able to boast an unusually long reign, her tenure on the English throne spanning some 45 years. She had overseen some significant political successes that had incited celebration on a national scale: the illustrious defeat of the Spanish Armada in 1588, for example. These various factors rendered her funeral a decidedly important occasion, both in terms of its role as a fitting tribute to a long-reigning and successful queen and as a piece of reassuring theatre that filled the gaping void left behind in her absence.

Preparations for the queen's funeral began in earnest soon after her death, under the instruction of her successor James VI of Scotland – now I of England. Flanked by a sea of burning torches, Elizabeth's body was first taken from Richmond Palace and carried along the Thames to Whitehall in the quiet closeness of night, the barge transporting her corpse draped in swathes of black cloth. At Whitehall the queen lay in state in a coffin fitted with folds of purple velvet; in this repose she awaited her coming funeral, while at Westminster Abbey black cloth was hung around the west door in anticipation of the arrival of her funeral procession. Meanwhile, fabric for mourning garments was hastily distributed in many thousands of yards to all who were expected to play a part in the day's events. And there were to be a great many participants.

The most spectacular moment of Elizabeth's funeral was without doubt the magnificent procession that escorted her body to its final resting place within the quiet recesses of Westminster Abbey. The chronicler John Stow remarked of the occasion that, 'the City of Westminster was surcharged with multitudes of all sorts of people, in the streets, houses, windows, leads and gutters, that came to see the obsequy'. It was an escort in which rank meant everything. At the head of the procession came the Knights Marshals' men, tasked with clearing the processional route of obstructions and people, followed by 15 poor men and 260 poor women dressed all in black. A little behind marched four trumpeters heralding the approach of the Standard of the Dragon, which was borne by Sir George Bourchier, a Member of the Privy Council of Ireland. Then came the humblest of the queen's servants, including wine and wheat 'porters', bell ringers, and makers of 'spice-bags'. Another four trumpeters announced the passing of the Standard of the Greyhound, which floated along just behind them, and behind this striking emblem filed more servants of a slightly higher standing than those that had come before, including 'herbingers', tallow chandlers, and brewers.

Further down the procession strode more prominent figures, including 'Doctors of Physicke', the queen's chaplains, barons, bishops, earls, and marquesses, brought up by the Bishop of Chichester, who was to be the preacher at the funeral. The Great Embroidered Banner of England swam majestically through the air after four 'Sergeants of Armes', and only a few paces behind appeared in all its sumptuous glory the body of the queen herself, described as:

> 'The lively picture of her Highnesse whole body, crowned in her parliament robes, lying on the corps balmed and leaded, covered with velvet, borne on a chariot, drawn by four horses trapt in black velvet.'[1]

The lively picture of the queen refers to the lifelike effigy, fashioned from wax, which would have been positioned on top of Elizabeth's actual corpse. The use of wax models in the funeral processions of English royalty was a deep-rooted custom that had been observed since the days of medieval kings, but the practice would lose much of its significance and prominence as the seventeenth century reached its concluding years.

The tail end of Elizabeth's funeral procession was made up of 'Gentlemen Ushers' carrying white rods, followed closely by the chief mourner, the Marchioness of Northampton, whose train was carried by two countesses. And so, surrounded by an army of processing mourners

21. A section of the funeral procession of Elizabeth I in 1603, by an unknown artist. Horses swathed in black cloth and decorated with escutcheons pull the hearse bearing the body of the queen to Westminster Abbey. Her funeral effigy can be glimpsed through the collection of heraldic banners held aloft by mourners. Elizabeth's funeral was a sumptuous spectacle that set the tone for succeeding royal burials in seventeenth-century England.

of every rank imaginable, Queen Elizabeth I was borne to the Abbey in a regimented sea of black. Proceedings rounded off in a fairly modest way for a spectacle that had been like no other event in living memory. A eulogy was preached by the Bishop of Chichester, who had participated in the funeral procession, and as the coffin disappeared from view beneath the vaulted ceilings of Westminster Abbey, staves were snapped and thrown into the queen's grave after her corpse.

It was to be little under a decade before the next royal funeral occurred in England, yet this one would be quite different in nature from that of Queen Elizabeth's. For one thing, it was the funeral of the heir apparent to the throne, the eldest son of James I of the now incumbent House of Stuart, not the funeral of the king himself. For another, it acted as a solemn farewell to a young man who had been tragically cut down in his prime. Elizabeth I had at least lived to a ripe old age, and her passing, although a sad occasion, was not unexpected when it came. The premature death of Prince Henry shook the royal family to its very core. The athletic Prince of Wales began to show signs of illness in October 1612, at the sprightly age of just 18, but he was said to have ignored his symptoms for several weeks before he was finally rendered bedridden at the end of the month. John Chamberlain speculated that a fever concentrated in the prince's head was to blame, and that his hair had been shaved off and his head applied with newly killed cocks and pigeons in an attempt to save his life. Such treatment was to be inadequate. Henry was dead by the evening of 6 November.

The heartrending circumstances surrounding the occasion ensured that Henry's funeral would be a tribute on par with that staged for Elizabeth I in 1603. It is estimated that close to 2,000 people walked in the funeral procession of the late prince, including members of his own household and those of the various households of his family. Prince Charles, later King Charles I, was appointed chief mourner, and must have appeared a feeble little character amongst the sprawling pageantry and solemnity of the event, for he was only a 12-year-old boy at the time. Besieging him from all sides would have been the tell-tale markers of a seventeenth-century royal funeral conducted with no expense spared, including banners, trumpeters, horses, and copious numbers of mourners dressed all in black.

Queen Anne of Denmark, Prince Henry's doting mother, was overcome with grief at the death of her son, so much so that even three years later she could not bear to see her surviving male offspring, Charles, be made Prince of Wales in his place. The queen, suffice to say, was not long for this world. She died early in 1619, probably of dropsy, and so events were duly set in motion to execute another royal send-off. The planning stages of Anne's funeral were fraught with difficulties, mainly of a financial nature. John Chamberlain reported on 27 March that money for the ceremony was in short supply, forcing the day of the funeral to be pushed back until the end of April; by the twenty-fourth of that month a date had still not been agreed on. Word got out that the proposed funeral was too expensive to pay for, with the event expected to cost at least three times as much as the funeral of the late Queen Elizabeth. Things became so desperate, reported Chamberlain, that there was even talk of melting down Queen Anne's gold plate and 'putting it into coin'. Another proposition put forward was to pawn the queen's jewels and 'other movables'. Delays were lengthened further by religious tensions, with a handful of Catholic women airing their grievances at being nominated to partake as mourners in a Protestant funeral procession.

In the end, Queen Anne's funeral was regarded as a decidedly disappointing pageant, barely worth the myriad uncertainties and headaches it had caused in the lead-up to the event. Chamberlain described it as a 'drawling, tedious sight, more remarkable for number than for any other singularity'. There were the usual ranks of poor women in attendance, numbering 280 in total, and the servants of great lords too, but to Chamberlain every mourner – even the lords and ladies themselves – was dressed alike, and therefore collectively made for a rather 'poor show'. They came 'laggering all along, even tired with the length of the way and weight of their clothes, every Lady having twelve yards of broadcloth about her and the Countesses sixteen'. The hearse upon which the body of the queen was carried, however, was described as fair and stately, so there was at least something in the procession to be admired. The solemnities at Westminster Abbey were not completed until 6.00pm, by which time it had been a very long and sombre day. An overall assessment of the funeral, offered by Chamberlain, was that it had gone almost without a hitch, save for the falling masonry *en route* to the Abbey that had killed a young man.

James I, by now in his mid-fifties and struggling with unreliable health, must surely have been aware as his wife's body was carried into Westminster Abbey that the next royal corpse to be brought there would in all likelihood be his own. If such a thought did cross his mind, he would regrettably be proven right. James died six years later, on 27 March 1625, leaving the throne to his son and heir apparent, Prince Charles. The king had been suffering from dysentery at the time of his death, and it was this and a stroke that was said to have finished him off, although some suspected murder at the hands of his adulated favourite, the Duke of Buckingham. Whatever the circumstances surrounding the king's death, another royal funeral was now in prospect, the fourth of any note in 22 years, and it was time once again to begin preparations for a farewell that would eclipse any that had come before it.

James' body was taken from Theobalds Palace, a favourite country pile, and carried back to London in the intimate darkness of a Monday evening (mirroring the transportation of Elizabeth I's corpse), through Smithfields, Holborn, Chancery Lane, and the Strand, to Denmark House where it would lie in state until the day of his funeral. Chamberlain remarked that the convoy was 'well accompanied' by 'all the nobility of the town', including pensioners, officers, household servants, the lord mayor, and some aldermen of the city. The solemnity of the corpse's initial procession was purportedly blemished by a spell of bad weather, so that through the dark haze blanketing London only the outlines of coaches and the indistinct lights of flickering torches could be observed from afar. The funeral itself took place several weeks later on 7 May, and suffered no such shortcoming. According to the scrupulous Chamberlain, the day succeeded in being a formidable and very visible display of royal power and pomp, as was undeniably its intention. In the letter-writer's eyes it was the greatest funeral that 'was ever known in England'. Black garments had been distributed to more than 9,000 mourners, who were to be a part of the by now familiar funeral procession, and the funeral hearse at the centre of proceedings, partly designed by the great architect Inigo Jones, was greatly admired and even considered 'the fairest and best-fashioned that hath been seen'. Charles was made chief mourner, as he had been for his elder brother in that lamentable year of 1612; he followed the procession on foot, from Denmark House to Westminster Abbey, carefully parading himself in front of many thousands of onlookers as the undisputed new king and national figurehead of his late father's realms. By the time the colossal entourage had finished snaking its way into the Abbey it was 5.00pm, and very late indeed before the funeral sermon, two hours in length, and other ceremonial rites had concluded. Although an impressive sight, and costing in all around £50,000 to execute, Chamberlain could not help but comment in hindsight that the order was at times 'very confused and disorderly'. Clearly some people could never be wholly satisfied.

The reign of King Charles I was a troubled one, damaged by clashes with his recalcitrant Parliament, whom he famously did away with for 11 years between 1629 and 1640, and ultimately suppressed by a catastrophic civil war which ended in total disaster for the English monarchy. The exceptional nature of Charles' death in 1649 meant that his laying to rest, when it came, would be worlds apart from the considerable solemnity and pageantry observed at his father's funeral a quarter of a century earlier. Charged with high treason following the seven-year conflict with Parliament known to posterity as the English Civil War, Charles was put to death by beheading on a cold winter's morning in January, as we have already discovered. On the executioner's strike, successful in severing the king's head on the first attempt, the centuries-old English constitution was thrown into complete disarray. Kingship was effectively abolished.

Consequently, Charles' funeral was, by a king's standards at least, a small and discreet affair. It offered a tantalising flavour of the royal funerals of the early seventeenth century without being able to fully realise their unrivalled majesty and scale. William Juxon, the Bishop of London, and Sir Thomas Herbert, the deceased king's gentleman of the bedchamber, saw to it that Charles' body was coffined and covered with a black velvet pall straight from the scaffold. The corpse was embalmed soon afterwards. Next there was some disagreement over where exactly King Charles should be buried. Herbert insisted that the Henry VII Chapel, located in all its grandeur at the east end of Westminster Abbey, represented the perfect spot, for here lay the bodies of earlier monarchs and members of the king's own family, including Edward VI, Mary I, Elizabeth I, Mary, Queen of Scots, James I, and James' eldest son, Prince Henry. The Abbey was unsurprisingly denied by those 'that were then in power', the reason being that it would attract too much unwanted attention from the public. It was eventually decided that the king's body would be interred within the more secluded precincts of St George's Chapel at Windsor Castle.

With a burial location approved, Charles' corpse was duly carried to Windsor in a hearse covered with more black velvet, drawn by six horses that had likewise been draped in black. Four coaches rattled along behind the initial spectacle, conveying about 'a dozen gentlemen and others' out of London to Windsor in black garments, most of whom it was reported had waited on the king during his imprisonment at Carisbrooke Castle. Arriving at its destination, the royal corpse was carried through the Dean's House and placed in the king's usual bedchamber at Windsor Castle. Meanwhile, having assembled in the wake of Charles' death, a prominent band of noblemen deliberated over where in St George's Chapel to bury the body. As the search was conducted, one of the lords present was said to have experimentally beaten his staff against the stone pavement in the choir, causing a hollow sound to emanate from beneath the floor. An order was given to remove the various 'stones and earth' covering the ground, which revealed a vault housing two grand coffins, both adorned with velvet palls. It was supposed that these contained the bodies of King Henry VIII and his third wife, Jane Seymour. The discovery beneath the choir soon made up the minds of the indecisive searchers.

Charles' body was carefully removed from its temporary repose in the private quarters of Windsor Castle, and, after sitting for a little while longer in St George's Hall, the coffin was carried by gentlemen of 'some quality' to the west end of St George's Chapel. Circumstances dictated that the funeral procession was modest at best for a sovereign, with only a handful of lords, governors, and attendants following the corpse to its final resting place under the choir. The day's events, however, were regarded by some as entirely fitting, and even rather beautiful. The sky was said to have been 'serene and clear' at first, but then we are told it began to snow, coming down so fast that by the time the procession had reached the west end of the Chapel, the black velvet pall covering the coffin had turned 'all white': the colour of innocence. Leaving the thick sheets of snow outside, the king's bearers, followed by the procession, entered the Chapel quietly and purposefully, with no baying crowd or wailing audience to disturb them. Charles had died in a manner that was both violent and agonisingly public, but on his funeral day the tempest encircling his execution had all but blown away. He was able to have an intimate and peaceful interment.

Almost immediately after the extraordinary beheading of Charles I, concerted efforts were made to formally write the monarchy out of the English constitution. The remnants of the House of Commons

22. An 1877 drawing of the funeral of Charles I in 1649. The circumstances surrounding the king's death meant that his funeral was an unusually subdued affair, with only a modest procession accompanying his body to St George's Chapel at Windsor. Snow fell that day, which led some to speculate that it was a sign of his innocence.

came together in February 1649 and carried a resolution 'that it had been found by experience...that the office of a king...is unnecessary, burdensome and dangerous to the liberty, safety and public interests of the people of this nation, and therefore ought to be abolished'. As a result, a Council of State was duly set up to manage home and foreign affairs, headed by an eminent Parliamentarian and distinguished military leader named Oliver Cromwell. Cromwell had played a decisive role in the recent civil war and the unprecedented execution of the former king. It is one of history's great ironies that, in assuming the elevated status of Lord Protector of the newly established Commonwealth, Cromwell himself became a king in all but name. His funeral in 1658 was certainly evocative of a sovereign's, continuing in an assured manner the trend of unequalled pomp and solemnity, conducted on a huge scale, that had characterised the funerals of both Queen Elizabeth and King James. Indeed, in a time of great constitutional uncertainty, it was perhaps more important than ever before to showcase the authority and stability of the country's leadership through an extravagant state occasion.

It was the death of Cromwell's daughter, Elizabeth, on 6 August 1658, that triggered the rapid deterioration in the Lord Protector's own health. Soon it became apparent that he was also dying. Cromwell was perfectly aware of his impending demise, of course. He uttered knowingly in the last few weeks of his life that, 'I would be willing to be further serviceable to God and His people, but my work is done'. Death eventually came on 3 September, just under a month after the loss of Elizabeth, blamed at the time on a generic ague but now thought to have been the result of a deadly strain of malaria. Cromwell had been regarded as a monarch merely without the regalia in life, and in death there would be no difference in attitude. Just as he had lived like a king, he would also now be buried like one. In the usual ceremonial manner reserved for members of the English royal family, the Lord Protector's coffin was conveyed from Whitehall to Somerset House on the night of 25 September, where a lying-in-state would be observed until the day of the funeral. There was speculation that the coffin was in fact empty by the time it had embarked on its nocturnal journey through London. Contemporary reports indicated that the embalming process on the corpse had gone wrong, leaving Cromwell in such a sorry state physically that he had been deemed unsuitable for public exhibition, even when coffined. A commentator wrote:

> 'His body being opened and embalmed his milt was found full of corruption and filth, which was so strong and stinking, that after the corpse was embalmed and filled with aromatic odours, and wrapped in a 'cere-cloth', six double, in an inner sheet of lead, and a strong wooden coffin, yet the filth broke through them all, and raised such a noisome stink, that they were forced to bury him out of hand.'[2]

Whether or not this was mere hearsay or slander is up for debate, but what can be established with certainty is that Cromwell's body was buried in private at an undisclosed time before the day of the funeral. A wax effigy of the Lord Protector, which was to be displayed at his lying-in-state and carried to Westminster Abbey in the funeral procession, would at any rate do more than justice to the corporeal man.

Those wishing to view the initial lying-in-state were guided through four rooms hung with copious amounts of black velvet, the fourth being the most sumptuously and melancholically decorated of all, and containing the wax figure of Cromwell. The likeness could be found positioned beneath a large, black canopy, the bed supporting it surrounded by four pillars topped with beasts featured on the 'Imperial Arms', eight silver candlesticks aglow with lit tapers, and a suit of armour. The effigy itself communicated a powerful and unmistakable message of regality and kingly authority. It was dressed in a 'kirtle robe' of purple velvet, decorated with gold lace and trimmed with ermine fur, and draped over the top of this garment was a large, purple robe also finished with ermine fur, as well as 'rich' strings and gold tassels. Strapped around the kirtle was a 'rich embroidered' belt set with a 'richly gilt' sword. The wax hands poised on either side of the belt held aloft in the candlelight two important objects: in the right was a golden sceptre, 'representing government', and in the left could be discerned a globe, an emblem of 'principality'. Yet the most telling monarchical feature of all was to be located on a golden chair behind the reclining figure, for here, placed conscientiously atop a cushion, lay the Imperial Crown. By the time the effigy had begun its procession to the Abbey on

23. An 1877 drawing of Oliver Cromwell sitting with his daughter, Elizabeth Cromwell, as she succumbs to a terminal illness. The pair are shown holding hands.

The LORD PROTECTOR lying in State at Sommerset House.

Engraved by J.ª Caldwall, from the original print in the Collection of JOHN TOWNELEY ESQ.ᴿ

24. Oliver Cromwell's lying-in-state at Somerset House, London, in 1658, engraved by James Caldwell in the eighteenth or early nineteenth century. His lofty position as Lord Protector entitled him to a kingly death. This usually included an elaborate display of the regal coffin or effigy in the interim between the death of the monarch and his or her funeral. In Cromwell's case an effigy was placed in a room hung with black velvet, watched over by mourners. It is thought that Cromwell's body was buried many weeks prior to his funeral occurring.

23 November, the Crown would find itself positioned on the Protector's wax head for all to see.

The funeral procession of Oliver Cromwell was every bit as magnificent as the royal funeral parades that had predated the unfortunate reign of Charles I. The diarist John Evelyn thought that the day's offerings were nothing short of 'superb'. He recalled how Cromwell's effigy was carried from Somerset House in a 'bed of state' drawn by six horses, and noticed the Imperial Crown on the effigy's head, perceiving that it made the Lord Protector look like a king. Evelyn further remarked that, 'there was none but cried, but dogs, which the soldiers hooted away with a barbarous noise; drinking, and taking tobacco in the streets as they went'. Indeed, as much as this event was essentially billed as a royal funeral procession, it also possessed the unambiguous qualities of a military pageant, with soldiers in attendance all along the route and army officers assuming key roles in the glittering procession. Surrounding the carriage that supported the effigy, in prime position, were eight such officers, who held several pieces of Cromwell's armour in their arms, a further nod to the military significance of the occasion.

Many thousands of spectators turned out to pay their respects to Cromwell on that joyful November day in 1658. It was an enthusiasm for the Lord Protector that would not last long. Oliver's eldest son, Richard Cromwell, succeeded his father as Lord Protector on the former's death. It immediately became obvious that he lacked the skills necessary for the position that had been handed down to him. A series of disagreements with the New Model Army, who had been so faithful to the first Lord Protector, ultimately paved the way for Richard's resignation from office only nine months into his term. With the second and final Lord Protector withdrawing meekly from the national stage and the foundations of the Commonwealth noticeably buckling, calls were made to wipe the constitutional slate clean and reinstate the time-honoured English monarchy, which had now been absent in England for a decade.

On 29 May 1660 the Restoration of the monarchy was successfully achieved with the arrival of Charles I's son, now King Charles II, into London to widespread celebration. It was a political shift that swiftly served to sour the once respected Cromwell name. Richard Cromwell was able to live out the rest of his years quietly, living mainly abroad but returning to England towards the end of the century and dying in his eighties in 1712. Oliver's corpse was not so lucky. In January 1661 the carcasses of the late Lord Protector, John Bradshaw (the judge who had condemned Charles I to death), and the Protector's son-in-law, Henry Ireton, were 'dragged from their tombs' and taken to the gallows at Tyburn on the orders of Charles II, where they were strung up for several hours in a morbid demonstration of posthumous hanging before being taken down and decapitated. The headless corpses were buried in a deep pit below the gallows, while the rotten heads were taken to Westminster Hall to be exhibited on spikes. This was to be the men's punishment for having a hand in the death of the king's father. The gruesome exhumation was a far cry from the resplendent and reverential funeral held for Cromwell only two years before, and was enough to unravel everything that the Lord Protector's original burial had symbolised: adulation, authority, and above all, sovereignty. As John Evelyn wrote wryly after the event had taken place, 'look back at November 1658 and be astonished'.

The reign of Charles II stretched on for a quarter of a century before the king found himself on his deathbed in early 1685. The monarch's life began to ebb away on the morning of 2 February, when Charles rose early complaining that he had not slept well the previous night. Soon afterwards he collapsed, having suffered a suspected apoplectic fit. By 5 February, a Thursday, the king's doctors announced that he was dangerously ill. All manner of remedies had been administered to the dying sovereign in an attempt to save his life, including bloodletting and blistering agents, provoking some to liken the room in which the king lay to a torture chamber. Although a few had temporarily relieved Charles of his symptoms and had on one occasion returned his speech to him, in the end they were none of them to any avail. Charles II died at the age of 54 on 6 February, a mere four days after he had first been taken unwell. Before the rattle came, he had controversially renounced his Protestant faith and was received into the Catholic Church.

The king's funeral occurred, for the standards of the time, relatively soon after his decease. John Evelyn was underwhelmed by proceedings, observing that on the night of 14 February the king was 'very obscurely buried' in a vault under the Henry VII Chapel in Westminster Abbey 'without any manner of pomp'. There were murmurs in London that the discreet nature of Charles' obsequies was a result of his conversion to Catholicism, although it later transpired that the king was buried 'according to the liturgy of the Church of England'. Nonetheless, Gilbert Burnet, who would later become Bishop of Salisbury, concurred with Evelyn that the funeral was a 'mean' affair, that the expense of it was considerably less than the average nobleman's burial, and that the late king deserved better from his brother, the newly reigning monarch James II.

That the funeral was held at night may have misled contemporary writers into believing that the ceremony was more low-key than was actually the case, although it is highly possible that the occasion did embrace a sense of intimacy not present at the burials of monarchs earlier on in the century. As has been mentioned already, a nighttime funeral allowed for a more personal and private atmosphere. In actual fact, Charles II's obsequies were said to have followed all the usual conventions of a sovereign's death and funeral, commencing with a lying-in-state, complete with royal effigy, and culminating in a nocturnal procession to Westminster Abbey. King James and his wife, Queen Mary of Modena, were in attendance, as was Prince George of Denmark – the husband of King James' daughter, Princess Anne – who assumed the role of chief mourner. The trials endured by the English monarchy in the middle years of the seventeenth century meant that Charles' was the first interment of a monarch in Westminster Abbey for 60 years, since the burial of his grandfather James I in 1625. The Abbey's next royal interment, the last of the century, would come around much faster.

James II's hold on the English crown was short-lived. Being an open Roman Catholic in a Protestant country ultimately lost him his throne, and in 1689 he was replaced by his son-in-law, William of Orange, and William's wife, the ex-king's eldest daughter, Princess Mary. They would rule jointly for just under six years as William III and Mary II, until smallpox robbed William of his queen prematurely in December 1694. The manner of Mary's death was all the more tragic because she had been struck down with the illness once before and miraculously survived. Upon the second contraction of smallpox her luck had run out. William was said to have been left broken by the loss of his wife at the age of just 32. With the king's sorrow came an outpouring of genuine anguish from the nation, who had held the late queen in high esteem and shown her particular affection because she was English. Now a Dutchman remained as the sole ruling monarch in a foreign land and the country was left bereft.

Mary II's funeral was to be hugely impressive, the likes of which had probably not been seen for a monarch since the obsequies observed for Elizabeth I almost a century before. It certainly easily outstripped the nighttime solemnities of Charles II's burial in the 1680s. Some argue that the exemplary pomp and ceremony of the queen's funeral, which was held on 5 March 1695, merely constituted a clever piece of propaganda intended to strengthen the legitimacy of both Mary's and particularly William's claim to the throne, the latter being a notoriously unpopular ruler. Those less sceptical and present on the day might have viewed the solemnities as an appropriate farewell to a highly respected monarch.

Mary's lying-in-state was set up in a room at Whitehall Palace hung with purple velvet, the colour of royalty, with 'large wax tapers' scattered across the floor and veiled ladies of the bedchamber positioned at the four corners of the queen's bed, performing a devoted vigil. More veiled maids were attendant in an antechamber finished with purple cloth, and in another room were to be found pages dressed in black. The king invited members of Parliament to wear mourning clothes and to take part in the funeral procession, an oddity that no doubt added to the pageantry and uniqueness of that March day. The frail King William himself did not attend the funeral. The procession was without question an admirable affair, being the perfect blend of solemn observance and theatrical performance, which was embodied most perceptibly in the long line of mourners who filed from Whitehall to Westminster Abbey. The verdict of the traveller Celia Fiennes reinforces the impressive quality of Queen Mary's funeral and the great impact it clearly had on the watching masses, she observing confidently that the king 'omitted no ceremony of respect to her memory and remains'. Evelyn, too, thought that the funeral must have been 'infinitely expensive', for never had there been 'so universal a mourning':

> 'All the Parliament-men had cloaks given them, and 400 poor women; all the streets hung, and the middle of the street boarded and covered with black cloth. There were all the Nobility, Mayor, Aldermen, Judges, &c.'[3]

If Evelyn is to be believed, then such an eccentric display was not what Mary II had in mind for her obsequies at all. Private papers left behind by the queen supposedly requested that her funeral should not amount to any 'extraordinary expense'. Her modest wishes, however, were discovered too late in the day to be effected, and so there was instead no expense spared.

The procession having entered the Abbey, the customary funeral sermon was preached, during which Queen Mary's body was 'reposed in a mausoleum in the form of a bed', finished with black velvet and a 'silver fringe'. Hanging in the mausoleum's arches and placed at its four corners were tapers of an undisclosed type, perhaps cradling small flames. In the middle of the structure a basin supported by the shoulders of cupids held a 'great lamp' that burned throughout the service.

25. The lying-in-state of Mary II of England in 1695, etched by John Overton. The queen is surrounded by purple velvet, columns, and lit tapers. Her ladies of the bedchamber perform a devoted vigil.

Fiennes reported that the sermon was accompanied by 'solemn and mournful' music, and singing too, reverberating around the cavernous Abbey to the same rhythm as the flames that flickered in the centre of the mausoleum. Finally, before the sealing of the tomb, white staves were snapped by the queen's officers and thrown into the royal grave, symbolising that their service to her was done, just as had happened at the burial of Queen Elizabeth in the same Abbey 92 years before. Then the tomb was sealed, and the last royal funeral to be held in seventeenth-century England was over. The similarities between Queen Mary's funeral in 1695 and Queen Elizabeth's in 1603 show just how little the funeral rites of English royalty changed over the course of the century, on those occasions when royal obsequies could indeed be expressed freely and openly. As was underlined at the beginning of this chapter, royal funerals were like little else observed in the insular world of pre-industrial England. They strove to impress, and this is what ultimately made them one-of-a-kind events.

Chapter 8

The Unorthodox Burial

'Mens bones were Plowd up in my Stone-hill Close, & upon enquiry of ye old inhabitants & search of ye register I found they were like to be some of ye Armitages, six of whom dyed of ye Sickness & were buryed there in the year 1631.'[1]

In 1684, as described above, the clergyman William Sampson reported that skeletal remains had been ploughed up in an unusual spot near his house in Clayworth, Nottinghamshire. His surprise at the discovery led him to make some enquiries about how the bones had ended up there. A mixture of local records and native knowledge drew the conclusion that they belonged to members of the ill-fated Armitage family, who had been buried in the field 50 years earlier.

There were a variety of reasons why some were not given a so-called normal burial in seventeenth-century England. In the case of the Armitages, infectious disease was to blame, specifically plague. Fears of contamination during outbreaks left parish officials with little choice but to insist that victims were disposed of away from the consecrated spaces of churches and churchyards. Makeshift graves in fields and gardens were sometimes the only viable option for a sick household, particularly in the countryside. In 1665, in Wilmslow, Cheshire, a woman recorded merely as E. Stonaw was buried in her garden because it was suspected that she had died of the plague, she having only come home the day before. Some years before, in 1647, Robert Lenthall of Great Hampden was forced to bury his daughter by a hedge after she succumbed to the disease while paying her parents a visit, having picked it up in London. 'In ye Evening we buried her in ye meade called ye Kitchenmeade by ye hedgeside as you go downe into it on yor left hand, a little below ye pond', Lenthall wrote afterwards. She was only 14 years old. In one astonishing episode a soon-to-be casualty of the plague premeditated his unconventional burial in Cheshire by digging the grave with his own hands, nearby to where he lived, and settling himself down in it to die. The exact circumstances of the incident were noted in the Malpas parish burial register in 1625:

> 'Richarde Dawson…being sick of the plague and perceyving he must die at yt tyme, arose out of his bed, and made his grave, and causing his nefew, John Dawson, to cast some strawe into the grave, which was not farre from the house, and went and layed him down in the sayd grave, and caused clothes to be layd uppon, and soe dep'ted out of this world; this he did because he was a strong man and heavier than his said nefew and another wench were able to burye.'[2]

Dawson was trying to be helpful given the gravity of the situation, but his actions were nonetheless perplexing. To the modern looker-on his behaviour is very difficult to comprehend.

Plague burials occurred in unusual places in London too. During the shattering visitation of 1665 Samuel Pepys observed graves being dug on the banks of the River Thames. With some disdain, he also referred to the burial of more plague dead in the open fields around the capital. It was not so much anxiety over contagion that brought about interment in places other than churches or churchyards in plague-ridden London, but lack of space. So many Londoners died during epidemics that it was not always possible to get everybody buried within the confines of hallowed ground. Pepys' was alarmed by the sight of so many fresh graves piled on top of each other in the churchyard of St Olave, Hart Street, in January 1666. One notorious way in which the authorities attempted to solve this unwelcome urban problem was to sanction the excavating of pits for mass burials. The need became most urgent upon the eruption of plague in the spring of 1665, which spread like wildfire and claimed lives even faster. In August plague pits had already been dug in the parishes of St Dunstan-in-the-West and St Bride's; by the early months of 1666 it is probable that every major parish in the capital had followed suit. The pits conserved space and ensured that humble victims could continue to be buried in churchyards. While parishioners could take solace in this small mercy, the prospect of being pitched into a yawning chasm with hundreds of other fouled bodies might have been a difficult pill to swallow. It added insult to injury that those who were destined for the pits would probably be carried to them in a body collector's cart, smothered by other stinking corpses and announced to the rest of the city through the harsh calls of the collector for other cadavers. So much for a decent funeral procession.

Daniel Defoe developed a strange obsession with plague pits in his *Journal of the Plague Year*, published many years after the events of the Great Plague of London in 1722. The journal was probably based on a family diary, as Defoe was only a young boy at the time of the sickness. It most likely took artistic license and contained literary embellishments, but it is nevertheless a valuable and graphic account of the 1665 visitation. The narrator described the pit dug in the parish of Aldgate with awe and dread. When finished in early September, he reckoned it to be 40 feet long, 16 feet across, and 20 feet deep. The hole, in fact, extended down so far that excavators had run across water at the bottom, which stopped them from digging further. According to Defoe, 50 or 60 people might be put into one pit before it was closed up. As the death toll mounted, holes were made larger and this figure could rise to several hundred. In just two weeks the 'dreadful Gulph' at Aldgate had been filled with the bodies of over a thousand people. At this point, Defoe tells us, parish officials were required to cover it over, for there was an order in place decreeing that bodies were not to be buried within six feet of the surface of the churchyard. The journal's narrator decided to visit the pit at night when bodies were brought to the site and 'thrown' in, even though strictly speaking outsiders were forbidden from coming anywhere near the pits because of the risk posed by infection. Defoe believed it became even more imperative to avoid these spots as the plague advanced. Such was the desperation of the times in the capital that diseased persons took to flinging themselves into trenches wrapped in nothing but blankets or rugs, telling anybody who came near them, with a typical air of delirium, that they wished to get the inevitable over with. An open, unwalled pit in the parish of Cripplegate was regarded as a popular destination for hyperactive victims looking for an easy burial. It must be remembered that London was by no means alone in resorting to burying the plague dead in one grave if circumstances became bad enough. Ten bodies were buried together in a hut as far out as Rutland in October 1665.

Visions of the plague dead being buried could haunt the mind long after the disease had slipped into the pages of history. Samuel Newton was still having nightmares about such burials in the 1690s. By this point a significant outbreak of plague had not been seen in England for 30 years. In 1695 he wrote, with a no doubt trembling hand:

> 'Thursday night I dreamed, that I being in London, there came along Bishopsgate street almost the whole breadth of the street a great many persons haveing along with them a great many dead corps dyeing (as they said) of the plague in plaine coffins not of a black but of a sad couller and the covers not coped but flatt every corps not being borne on their shoulders, but borne *below* by 2 persons one at the head and the other at the feet who by the cord at each end not above a foot from the ground bore the corps along haveing noe hearscloath but the bare flatt coffin, these corps were borne along close one by another as many as tooke upp the full breadth of Bishopsgate and entred into and under to goe through that gate, and abundance of people followed the corpses to goe out through the gate which was throng'd and I my selfe being then to goe through that gate made some offer, but findeing by the croud it to be very hott and not easily to be passed and besides haveing a fear uppon mee and sadnas at that dismall sight, I turned downe not that street that leades to Moregate I being then on the other side of the way and soe turned downe that Lane by the gate that leades the way by London Wall to Algate and soe my dreame ceased leaving sadnes upon my spiritt...'[3]

Newton was clearly much affected by his experiences, to the point where he was unable to rid himself of them.

Concerning plague interments, even worse than a mass burial was no burial at all. On 22 August 1665, in the thick of disease, Pepys wrote in his diary:

> 'I went away and walked to Greenwich, in my way seeing a coffin with a dead body therein, dead of the plague, lying

125

in an open close belonging to Coome farme, which was carried out last night, and the parish have not appointed any body to bury it; but only set a watch there day and night, that nobody should go thither or come thence, which is a most cruel thing: this disease making us more cruel to one another than if we are doggs.'[4]

The same negligence was occasionally seen in England when it came to the disposal of the bodies of men who had died fighting in armed engagements. During the civil war, following a skirmish at Cirencester in 1643, the Eastcheap chronicler Nehemiah Wallington claimed that Parliamentary corpses had been left to rot above ground for at least four days in the town because nobody dared bury them sooner. It is possible that a number of rebels killed during the Battle of Sedgemoor in 1685 were never found in the fields of corn where they had fallen.

Combatants who perished fighting in an encounter were invariably treated to indecorous burials if their bodies were left at the mercy of the opposing force. As with plague victims, pits were often favoured for the interment of the enemy's dead, the difference being that whereas in times of epidemic disease the practice was viewed as an altogether necessary measure, during outbreaks of conflict mass burial could well be considered a deserved slight. The common soldier Adam Wheeler estimated that around 174 rebel corpses had been assembled in a heap to be buried in a pit near Weston, Somerset, in 1685. They had fought against their own sovereign at Sedgemoor, and therefore under no circumstances were they to be treated to a classic Christian burial. The victors would instead arrange for the traitors to be crammed together in a single grave, which alone would rob them of a fair amount of dignity, and they were also to be laid to rest in unconsecrated ground. The latter especially was a huge dishonour for sincere men who had expected all their lives to be decently committed to the earth within the comforting and sacred confines of a churchyard. Several days later local residents would complain that the rebels' bodies had not been sufficiently covered on the moorland where they had been deposited, leaving an offensive stink in the air. To deal with the problem, and on the instructions of King James II himself, ploughmen and horses were sent to the site to construct a larger mound.

Cavalier and Roundhead propagandists made it their mission to emphasise the cruel treatment of each side's war dead during the English

Civil War. The endless and blatant exhibitions of one-upmanship in the 1640s make it tricky to separate fact from fiction, and even for contemporaries it would have been a tall order to work out exactly what the truth of a report was. Nehemiah Wallington was a serial Roundhead exaggerator, bent on tarnishing the reputation of the king's supporters, but it would be ill-advised to dismiss his reports entirely. The capture of the town of Marlborough by Royalists in 1642 caused him to make a string of accusations against his foes:

> 'The number of their slain and wounded men they kept from our sight and knowledge as much as they could, but they had slain, as is conceived, above two hundred men. Many they buried the next day in the Town, and many they buried in several places in the fields about the Town. Some they threw into a very deep well, three furlongs from the Town, and many they carried away in carts, some say four or five loads, and cast in a river in their way.'[5]

According to Wallington, fields, wells, and rivers were considered suitable locales for Parliamentary graves following the encounter. He would make a far bolder claim after the siege of Hopton Castle in 1644. The fortress was a Roundhead stronghold until Sir Michael Woodhouse and a 500-strong Cavalier army captured it in the spring of that year. Having fallen to the king's men, Wallington maintained that the castle's defenders had been buried alive by their captors. Matthew Carter, quartermaster general in the Royalist ranks, added paraffin to the flames in 1648 when he bragged about the supposed treatment of Fairfax's late men at the siege of Colchester. 'Many of their dead bodies were thrown into wells', he wrote in an account of the event that reeked of propaganda, 'some buried in ditches, others were carried off, and considerable numbers were left behind'.

As the English Civil War accelerated, killing military personnel in their thousands, we know with certainty that out of sheer convenience soldiers from both armies were sometimes buried in mass graves on battlefields. A frantic search was launched for the corpse of Sir Edmund Verney after it was discovered that he had died fighting at the Battle of Edgehill in 1642. His son Ralph quickly established to his great dismay that, 'there is noe possibillity of finding my Deare father's Body', with a servant in the Earl of Essex's army informing him that it was likely Sir Edmund's body had been 'buried in the feilds'. A friend of the family's, Lady Sussex, was greatly unsettled by the revelation. 'My soro is beyonde all that can bee sade', she commented, 'but truly it trubles me much that his body was beriede amonst the multitude; I know itt coulde not have addede anythinge to him, only have sattisfiede his frindes to have hade a cristan beriall; but itt semes in war ther is no differince made'. She was right in thinking this. The practical disposal of the war dead frequently entailed the casting aside of normal, Christianly notions of interment, particularly where common graves were concerned. The Earl of Essex had shown a little more respect in 1643 following the First Battle of Newbury, when the picturesque parish of Enborne had quite literally been reduced to a bloody mess. He issued an order to the churchwardens requesting that they deal with the dead in whatever way they saw fit. Even then the Newbury causalities were buried in several impersonal tumuli, on a section of the battlefield known as Wash Common.

Religious beliefs were a major factor in determining whether an individual qualified for a standard burial in this period. Anybody who refused to acknowledge the established Church of England was at risk of an unconventional interment by default. Openly-practicing Catholics found themselves being recurrently shunned by members of the Church of England, many of whom believed that, as excommunicate persons, followers of the old faith should not be entitled to burials within the holy perimeters of Protestant churchyards and churches. In September 1684 John Richardson of Framwelgate was denied a church burial in Durham Cathedral because of his Catholic leanings. His grave had already been opened in the choir when the Bishop of Durham dramatically halted proceedings, ordering it to be covered over again. Richardson's body was subsequently committed to the earth in his own garden. In 1690 Mrs Richardson chose to be buried beside her husband in their little slice of paradise.

Catholic persecution had been much more rigorous earlier on in the century. When it was hatched in 1605, the Gunpowder Plot encouraged fresh waves of antipathy towards the Church of Rome and its heretical English champions, resulting in the widespread rejection of Catholic cadavers for several years afterwards. According to the Royalist William Blundell, writing in 1655, Protestant resistance was especially bad in Lancashire during his grandfather's time:

'In ye yeare 1611 a bitter storm of persecution extended its fury in these parts to ye bodyies of deceased Catholicks. The Churches in all places denied them burial; som were laid in ye fields, som in gardens, and others in high-wayes, as it chanced. One of thes (as I have heard it credibly reported) being interred in a common lane, had her corps pull'd out by ye hoggs, and used accordingly.'[6]

Blundell's grandfather, also William, hit back at the actions of local Protestant clergy by providing Catholics with their own burial ground in Little Crosby, known as 'the Harkirk'. Here those of the old faith could be interred decently and with respect, and most importantly within a religious setting. The ground itself was already considered consecrated when Blundell set it aside for the purpose. The Lancashire landowner would be hauled before the court of Star Chamber and fined £2,000 for this illegal undertaking, but it probably mattered very little to him. He had created a space where his own brethren could be put to rest without fear of harassment, and that was priceless. The first burial took place at the Harkirk in April 1611. William declared beforehand:

'I, William Blundell of Litle Crosbie, within the Countie of Lancaster, Esquire, a weeke or a fowertnighte before Christenmas laste paste, havinge hearde that Catholicke Recusants were prohibited to bee buried at theire Parishe Church, bethought mee (myself through God's grace beinge also a Catholique) where were best to make readie in this my village of Litle Crosbie a place fitt to burie suche Catholiques either of myne owne howse or of the Neighbourhoode as should depte this lyfe duringe the tyme of these trobles. And so I caused a litle peece of grownde to bee enclosed within myne owne demaine land in a place called of ould tyme… the Harkirke.'[7]

William Mathewson, a tenant of Blundell's and an ardent Catholic, was the first person to be brought to the Harkirk for burial, the parson of Sefton having turned away the funeral party when they arrived expectantly at the church gates with his corpse in 1611. Amazingly, the ground was still being used in 1700. The priest Thomas Eccleston was buried at the Harkirk with due decency in this year, after spending more than 40 years 'assisting poore Christians in ye parishes of Halsall and Aughton'.

The saying goes that God loves a trier, and there were certainly several valiant attempts to bury overt Catholics properly within the grounds of a parish church over the course of the century. Some efforts paid off. Burying the dead man or woman in secret in the night was a safe bet, as in the example of Rose Lunford of North Elmham in Norfolk, who, being a 'recustant papist', was successfully buried in North Elmham churchyard under the cover of darkness in 1642. Stripping the occasion of its religious appurtenances might persuade the minister himself to allow the burial to proceed, if he was feeling generous. In 1602 the recusant Thomas Cletheray of 'the North blockhouse' was 'put into his grave in drypoll churchyard...without the minister and without the order of buriall, according to lawe'. The papist Jaine Claurance was buried in the chancel of the church of St Martin Coney Street in York without any obvious opposition at all in 1670. This was a sign of the changing times perhaps. Brute strength was resorted to in 1605 to get Alice Wellington of Allenmoor, near Hereford, into her grave in the churchyard there. Her body was refused entry by the curate of Allenmoor on the grounds that she was a papist, sparking a popular disturbance that became so vicious that the Bishops of Hereford and Llandaff were forced to flee the scene. Civil officers were beaten off by Wellington's friends in their unswerving quest to see Alice buried properly, and in the end they were able to put her into the ground in the churchyard by force. Other attempts to bury Catholics, however, ended in resolute failure. Either the burial was thwarted before it could occur, which is what happened with the unlucky Mr Richardson, or graves were dug up and the body ousted when the truth had been revealed. We hop across the border at this point to Denbighshire in Wales. Lieutenant Williams got away with being buried in Llangollen churchyard for 10 days in 1681 before the penny dropped that there was a Catholic man lying amongst the dead. His body was removed immediately and deposited in Williams' garden by friends. You might say that the man who exhumed the corpse came off worse than the corpse itself on this occasion. There was no coffin to be found when the hole had been dug, just Williams' putrefying body, fused with the damp earth around it. The state of it was so bad that the sexton fell sick afterwards.

Protestantism ushered in a new generation of religious dissenters in seventeenth-century England. Nonconformists (as they were principally known after the Restoration of the monarchy in 1660) were Protestants who chose to break away from the established Church of England and embrace an alternative set of godly ideas and practices, usually in line with up-and-coming Protestant sects, such as those of the Baptists, Methodists, and Quakers. Dissenting groups were widely condemned by the Church of England following the Act of Uniformity of 1662, leading to many guilty ministers being sidelined from public life. As a result, the interment of nonconformists was not always straightforward. In fact it very rarely was. We have a particularly good record of the Quaker situation in the second half of the century, where members were routinely barred from partaking in the burial practices that most took for granted. The atmosphere of suspicion surrounding them was typified in 1653 on the burial of Richard Cockerell of Hackness in Yorkshire, after which it was observed by a parish record keeper that there 'was many of them they call Quaker' in attendance. Heated religious debate purportedly broke out at the graveside that day. The corpse of the wife of John Elams of Halifax, who had died in childbirth, was refused access to the local churchyard in 1678 because she had identified as a Quaker while alive. It is not clear from Oliver Heywood's account where the body was instead taken, but we know that in the same year and place Mr Henry Wadsworth, 'a great Quaker', was buried in his garden at the age of 66. Parish registers across the country suggest that Quaker burial grounds became a common feature of towns in the late 1600s, being successors to the Harkirk in their own right. An entry in the 1676 register for the parish of St Michael le Belfry in York disclosed that Catherine Todd, daughter of a Mr John Todd, was 'buryed in the quakers burying place'. In 1697 in London it was likewise recorded that Hannah Parker, servant to the watchmaker Daniel Quare, was 'carried to the Quakers ground in Cripplegate to be buried'.

To take one's own life in seventeenth-century England was considered fundamentally contrary to the laws of God. Those who had the audacity to commit suicide in this period were therefore treated harshly by the Church, which manifested in their bodies being prohibited from enjoying a consecrated burial. Traditionally suicides were buried at crossroads on the outermost reaches of a village or town, as far away from the physical heart of the community as possible. The body of Katharine Smith of West Hallam in Derbyshire was taken to be interred 'in ye crosse ways near ye wind mill' in 1698, after coroners ruled that she had killed herself. In 1692, coroners reached the same conclusion in Marsden, Yorkshire, after a woman had been found with her throat cut there. It was ordered that she be buried 'at a lane end in Lingarths'. Sometimes a suicide was buried close to where he or she had committed their unspeakable crime. In Derby in 1620 a prisoner who had jumped to his death from a bridge rather than face the dreadfulness of a gaol cell was interred 'on the highway side close at the foote of the bridge'. Detained persons who took their own lives while in custody might be buried in the gaol grounds as punishment for their actions; alternatively, if they had already been condemned to die, the detainee's corpse might be taken to the site of the foiled execution and interred there. The latter occurred when the would-be assassin of Oliver Cromwell, Miles Sindercombe, poisoned himself before his scheduled hanging in 1657, to the utter fury of his prosecutors. The scene was set and the gallows erected at Tower Hill on the day of Sindercombe's planned execution in February. All that was missing was the criminal to be hanged, and he would continue to be absent, for when the guard came to Sindercombe's chamber to bring him to the scaffold he found him dead in his bed. Edward Hyde, Earl of Clarendon in his *History of the Rebellion* thought he knew what had happened. Hyde recalled that Miles had been paid a farewell visit at the Tower the previous night by his sister, alleging that he was seen by guards then present rubbing his nose with his hand in a most peculiar manner as the siblings spoke together at the bedside. Once she had departed, Sindercombe allegedly removed his clothes, tucked himself under the sheets, and declared, 'this is the last bed I should ever go into'. During the night he sneezed once, but apart from that he remained unnervingly still for somebody who was about to be put to death for the failed assassination of the great Lord Protector. Following the discovery of his body physicians were called in to open up Sindercombe's head. Clarendon wrote:

> 'They found he had snuffed up through his nostrils some very well prepared poison, that in an instant curdled all his blood in that region, which presently suffocated him.'[8]

The insinuation was that Miles' sister had provided her brother with a lethal substance that would spare him from the horror of the gallows the next day. In the eyes of the Church and the law this was obnoxious behaviour on the part of both Sindercombes. Clarendon continued that Miles' body was 'drawn by a horse to the gallows where he should have hanged, and buried under it, with a strake driven through him, as is usual in the case of self-murders'.

There existed a growing appreciation in early modern England that people might not always be of sound mind, or even fully conscious, when they committed suicide, and thus were not wholly responsible for their actions. Miles Sindercombe knew what he was doing in 1657, but perhaps the Dane Martin Roseenstand in 1674 did not. In Oxford on Candlemas Day he was found hanged and naked in a privy house near the town's theatre, to which he had retreated in the early hours of the morning, never to be seen alive again. The jury considering the case were inclined to believe that he had hanged himself in his sleep, but other analysts were more sceptical. Much of the available evidence indicated that Roseenstand had been completely *compos mentis* when he had stripped naked, scurried down to the privy house with a candle to light his way, looped a cravat about his neck twice, and tied the noose to a rafter in the ceiling. The knee-jerk response of Roseenstand's brother upon finding the corpse was incriminating for a start. He had immediately taken the body down from the beam where it hanged and covered over his sibling's 'privities' with a coat, claiming to the authorities when questioned that Martin had expired while sitting on the toilet, probably from an abscess. This tall tale was in any case invalidated on inspection of the cadaver by a surgeon, who located bruising around Roseenstand's neck. Even more damning, though, was Martin's choice of reading material on the night of his death, which related to scriptural men who had half-hanged themselves to see what it would feel like. Whereas the jury argued that the subject matter more than likely led to lively dreams, inciting an innocent case of sleep-hanging, cynics such as Anthony Wood proposed that Roseenstand had been inspired to follow the example of his biblical predecessors while perfectly awake and lucid. The trouble was that it had gone wrong. Whether the man had consciously or unconsciously hanged himself, the uncertainty of the act meant that he was granted a stripped-down burial in the churchyard of St Mary Magdalen, 'close under the wall next to the stile or passage opposite to the Katherine Wheele gate'.

Some executed felons were ordered to be buried where they had been hanged or decapitated in seventeenth-century England, if, of course, they were not chosen to be dissected. This functioned as an extension of the criminal's punishment, an undertaking intended to humiliate, as well as acting as a deterrent to other prospective lawbreakers. We have already seen this procedure in action when it came to the unorthodox interment of Miles Sindercombe. According to the vicar John Rous, the remains of the Jesuit Arthur Gohogan, hanged for uttering treasonous words against Charles I, were dealt with in the same fashion in the 1630s:

> 'His quarters and heade being brought to Newgate, there came a letter to bury them, before they were hanged up, so that there was some doubt made where; but at length Mr. Atturny was sent to the King to knowe, and by his advice (for they bury none of us among them, &c.) the carkase was buried under the very place at Tiburne where he was hanged.'[9]

This was not a rule set in stone, however, and leniency towards the bodies of felons was shown on many occasions. Being a distinguished member of society helped. The Catholic courtier Edmund Coleman's body, in bits by the time it had undergone the savage ritual of hanging, drawing, and quartering, was distributed amongst his friends for burial in 1678. Coleman had been accused of being involved in the Popish Plot of the late 1670s. The courtesy bestowed on the esquire reached down to the meaner sort too. The son of a barber, Robert White, sentenced to die for stealing a clock and some clothes, was cut down from the noose after an hour and a half of hanging in 1692 and allowed to be taken to his mother's house in Oxford. White's popularity caused him to be carried to a nearby church so that as many people as possible could view his body. Attempts to revive him were made, but they were to prove fruitless. A few days later he was given a very respectable burial indeed, in which his coffin was supported by several young men and covered in a sheet held up by 'maides in white', and followed by more maids, women, and children. Best of all, even as a convicted felon he was permitted to be buried in the churchyard of All Saints, Oxford. The emphasis on the colour white at Robert's funeral was probably used to symbolise his innocence, as well as his youth.

In shadier episodes it was the criminal themselves who could be responsible for the orchestration and carrying out of an unorthodox burial in seventeenth-century England. Murderers might go to extreme lengths to cover up their crimes and escape the gallows, which involved depositing victims wherever was most inconspicuous or out of the way. In 1634 the Cheshire vicar Edward Burghall reported that a woman had killed her own daughter then, with the help of her son, buried the girl in a pit. Most examples from the century unfortunately centre on parents wishing to conceal the fact that they had murdered their bastard child or children. In 1662, Henry Newcome related from Manchester:

> 'After supp: I went to Mr Lightbowne's: & there wee heard of the sad wickednes that is comitted of the man that hath now a 2nd bastard by his servant. The childe is found buryed in the garden.'[10]

One could almost call a mother from Flintshire in Wales creative in her desperate bid to bury her bastard infant under a heap of stones in a churchyard in 1682. The child didn't stay buried for long, and the mother was eventually executed.

Although most irregular burials could be explained away as a necessary preventative measure in times of disease, the product of religious or state retribution, or otherwise, there remained certain eccentric interments that were difficult to justify. In 1670 Anthony Wood remarked on the strange burial of the Countess of Marlborough, mother of the Earl of Marlborough who had died at sea during the Four Days' Battle in 1666. She was laid to rest in her garden under a turnip plot, between two boards, merely because she did not want one particular individual knowing that she was dead.

Chapter 9

Remembrance

'My wretched body to be beryed in my Charterhouse at Hulle, where y wol my ymage and stone be made and the ymage of my best beloved wyf by me, she to be there with me yf she lust, my said sepulture to be made by her discretion in ye said Charterhouse where she shal thinke best, in caas be yat in my dayes it be not made nor begonne.'[1]

Thus went the will of William de la Pole, Duke of Suffolk, in 1450. Suffolk's desire for his likeness to be posthumously evoked through the construction of a church monument shows that the English had been concerned with personal commemoration after death since the late medieval period and before. Remembrance practices were nothing new in the seventeenth century, therefore, but they were arguably more significant than they had been in medieval England. By the 1600s, the communities of the living and the dead had been wrenched apart to a degree unheard of in pre-Reformation times. The abolition of intercessory prayer in the sixteenth century, provoked by Protestant rejection of the doctrine of Purgatory, had helped to promote a peculiar sense of finality at the moment of death. Once somebody was dead, they were now truly gone. Methods of remembrance became especially important for a society that collectively feared the plunge into instantaneous, permanent obscurity. Memorialisation of the individualistic qualities of a person, in particular, was craved as it had never been before.

Elaborate monuments or tombs continued to be favoured by members of the nobility in seventeenth-century England as a way in which to be remembered following death's oblivion. Enshrined in the hallowed recesses of the parish church, these erections were chiefly commissioned to commemorate the social status and local influence of the late aristocratic man or woman, and to ensure that they retained a presence of authority in the parish long after their bodies had turned to dust.

Noble testators sometimes specified the kind of monument they wanted when writing their wills, just as William de la Pole had done over 150 years earlier. Some instructions were more exact than others. In 1631 Sir Hugh Myddleton, 'cittizen and gouldsmith of London', merely willed that a monument should be set up for him in St Matthew's Church at the discretion of his executrix. Sir William Cornwallis of Brome went into much more detail in 1611:

> '...my will and mynde is to have one Tombe or monument to be...made for my self with mention of both my wives (viz) of the Ladie Lucie my late wife Deceased...and of Dame Jane my nowe wife and of all my Children And alsoe one other Tombe or monument of plaine stone to be there likewise made and erected in the saide Chancell for my great Grandfather William Cornewaleis Esquire whoe lyeth buried there with a stone over him.'[2]

As is evident, there was as much a concern for the memorialisation of familial relationships as there was for the prominence of the individual testator in Cornwallis' directions. The Suffolk knight wanted his monument to commemorate the network of kinship that had surrounded him in life, and how he had been positioned within that network: first and foremost, he was the husband of two wives and the father of several children. With the addition of a new tomb for his ancestor nearby, he would also be remembered as the great-grandson of an esquire. Dame Anne Wingfield made a similar move in 1625, desiring in her will that she be buried in a tomb next to her first husband's in the parish church of Letheringham; the two monuments, sitting side by side, would work together to commemorate their prestigious marital union. We know that this is exactly what went on to happen. Through the observations of Robert Hawes, an early eighteenth-century steward of the Framlingham

Estate, it is confirmed that Dame Anne was duly buried in a tomb by that of her late husband's, as she had gone to great pains to request. It was described as 'a black marble stone plated with brass having the form of a woman with hands in praying posture delineated thereon'. Under the feet there was an inscription, memorialising in a simple way the Wingfields' earthly marriage:

> 'Here lieth the body of Lady Anne Wingfield…first married to Sir Anthony Wingfield of Letheringham […] She died the Second of August. Anno Domini 1626.'[3]

Regrettably the monument no longer exists, along with many others that were first planned in wills.

Surviving church monuments from the seventeenth century are on the whole successful in memorialising the aristocracy as high-status individuals as well as family members. The parish church of St Peter and St Paul in Kedington, Suffolk, is often described as the Westminster Abbey amongst village churches due to its unusually high number of monuments, including tombs and effigies. The effigy of Sir Thomas Barnardiston, a wealthy landowner who died in 1610, can be observed within its walls clad in decorative armour, the hands clasped piously against the breastplate, the head resting (surely uncomfortably) on a plumed helmet. Barnardiston's two wives kneel in prayer above him, capturing in sculpted stone, in a rather submissive pose it must be said, the nobleman's immediate family. However, the imposingness of the monument and its blunt imagery suggests that this was ultimately a display of superiority, both on a parish and familial level. The Alington monument found in All Saints' Church in Horseheath, Cambridgeshire, does an altogether better job of memorialising the personal relationships of the landed gentry in the seventeenth century. Importantly, it also brings to mind the grandeur of the Alingtons' circumstances and the foremost space they occupied in the village of Horseheath. Erected in 1613, the alabaster monument is somewhat faded nowadays, but at the time of its construction it would have been sumptuously painted and gilded, gleaming like a jewel in the otherwise whitewashed chancel. It remains an impressive piece of craftsmanship. The resplendent effigies of Sir Giles and Lady Dorothy Alington, one bedecked in a suit of armour and the other a fine dress, take centre stage. The couple's stateliness is unmistakable through the extravagant design of the structure, which extends up the chancel wall in a flourish of marble and finishes with an array of ancient crests. Yet there is very strong familial symbolism here too. Unlike Barnardiston's monument, in which his effigy is physically removed from those of his devoted wives, the statues of Lord and Lady Alington lie next to each other in their eternal rest, immortalising the close affiliation they shared in life as man and wife. The Alingtons are concurrently commemorated as parents at the base of the monument, where the carvings of six kneeling children are presented, one of which holds a death's head in its hands. The inscription cements the familial tone of the commemoration:

'Here resteth in assured Hope to rise in Christ Sir Giles Alington of Horseheath, Knight, accompanied with Lady Dorothy, his wife, Daughter of Thomas Earle of Exeter, Baron Burghley, and who made him a joyfull Father of tenne Children (Elizabeth, Thomas, Giles, James, Dorothy, Susan, Anne, Catherine, William and Mary), [who] ended this transitory life the 10th November 1613, to whose dear memory her sorrowful Husband mindful of his own mortality erected this monument.'[4]

One cannot ignore the religious mood of the Kedington and Horseheath monuments. The gestures of prayer displayed by each of the effigies implies a clear dedication to faith that both the Barnardistons and Alingtons hoped to isolate in representations of their future selves. It is only a shame that the likeness of Lady Dorothy no longer has hands.

Church monuments came in a variety of forms in seventeenth-century England. At the turn of the century alabaster or marble sculptures were all the rage, as we have already discovered in the above examples. They didn't come cheap though. The marble monument dedicated to the memory of the politician James Whitelocke, which still stands proudly in the church at Fawley in Buckinghamshire, cost the sizeable sum of £114 to make and paint in 1633. It could be a lengthy process. Sir Ralph Verney's monument for his deceased wife, which was to employ a mix of black marble, white marble, coloured marble, and alabaster, took several years to complete from the planning stages to the finished product in the 1650s. Sir Ralph launched the project before Mary's body was even

26. The tomb of Sir Thomas Barnardiston in Kedington church, Suffolk. It was erected following Thomas' death in 1610 and is a classic example of an early seventeenth-century church monument dedicated to a member of the English aristocracy.

cold. On her death in August 1650 he wrote to Dr William Denton straight away to instruct him to take measurements in the chancel of Middle Claydon parish church, and to mark where the monument was going to be erected. Denton was told to then describe his findings to an appropriate craftsman. 'Send me two or three draughts on paper drawne Black & White, or in Colours as it will bee', Ralph dictated, 'that I may see which Toombe I like best'. By 1651 it had been decided that the Frenchman Monsieur Duval should be entrusted with overseeing the creation of Mary's ornate tomb, with the work to be done at 'one of the best stonecutters' houses in London'. Ralph had a very clear idea of what he wanted the marble feature to look like. Writing to Dr Denton again on 23 September 1651, a year into the assignment, Verney described his vision for the anticipated masterpiece in obsessive detail:

> 'Now for a Tombe, ye chancell being little…I was thinking to make an Arch of Touch [black granite] or Black Marble; within the whole Arch shall bee black, & her statue in White Marble in a Winding sheet with her hands lift upp set upon

27. The two wives of Sir Thomas Barnardiston kneeling in prayer, almost submissively, above his effigy in Kedington church.

> an Urne or Pedestall uppon which or on ye edge of ye Arch may bee what Armes or Inscriptions shall bee thought fit. I was thinking to make a double Arch and in it to set upp her statue, & only leave a Pedestall for mine, for my sonn to set upp, if hee thinke fit, but I doubt this would bee thought vanity, being there is non for my Father & Mother, but if it please god to give me life & my estate, I will set up a tombe for them.'[5]

Six months later sketches were still being passed between Ralph and his designers, some of whom lived as far away as Rome. Mary had been dead for nearly two years by this point. Needless to say the monument would not be completed properly until the middle of the decade.

Monumental brasses were an economical type of sepulchral memorial installed in churches by the gentry, and the middling sort to an extent, in the seventeenth century. They had been popular since the medieval period and continued to be commissioned until the 1700s. It is estimated that a few thousand of these brasses still survive in the twenty-first century, including those pertaining to the Martin (or Martyn) family in Long Melford church, Suffolk. The handsome brasses are fixed to the stone floor of the south chancel aisle and might be missed entirely by the unaware visitor. On the right-hand side facing towards the tower is a fine-looking example from 1615, commemorating the esquire Roger Martyn, who died at the remarkable age of 89. He is dressed in a long gown and flanked by his two wives, Ursula and Margaret, who are wearing French hoods and ruffs. All three of them stand united in prayer on pedestals. Below these circular platforms is the modest inscription, identifying the man who has been depicted in brass and whose body lies beneath the dark slab, and further down there are two more miniature

28. A monumental brass depicting Roger Martyn and his family in Long Melford church, Suffolk, c.1615. Such monuments were a cheaper alternative to the alabaster memorials seen elsewhere and had been popular since the medieval period.

29. A second monumental brass in Long Melford church portraying Richard Martin, his wives, and his children, c.1624. The familial tone is particularly strong in this brass, as it includes images of two infants in swaddling clothes.

plates portraying the couple's children. On the left-hand side is a separate brass from 1624. The stress placed on family and hierarchy here is even greater, with the monument's central figure and subject, Richard Martin, surrounded by three elegantly outfitted wives, two infants in swaddling clothes, and two older sons, the younger of whom holds a skull to his chest. At least one other plate that made up the memorial has been lost, leaving a near-imperceptible imprint in the floor.

The passage of time brought with it changes to the intrinsic qualities of church monuments. Protestantism encouraged posthumous secular imagery to blossom. Physical death became more overtly represented in monumental designs in the later seventeenth century, as seen in the c.1660s wall memorial to Nathaniel and Jane Barnardiston inside Kedington church, where the two marble effigies, looking rather weary, each rest a hand on a skull. The late seventeenth-century Wentworth monument in the south aisle of the Lady Chapel in York Minster has a large and austere funeral urn as its centre, with the flowing figures of William Wentworth, Earl of Strafford, and his wife, Lady Henrietta, positioned on either side of it, seeming somehow to be cast in its shadow. The structure, columned and made of heavily veined marble, provides a flavour of the neoclassical architectural style that would take the upper classes by storm in the next century. The Wentworth monument is reflective of another development in the style of English memorials during the seventeenth century. Unlike the Barnardistons and the Alingtons of the 1610s, the Wentworths are standing up in their commemorative feature of the 1690s. This was a

30. A wall monument dedicated to Nathaniel and Jane Barnardiston, c.1660s. Their upright likenesses each rest a hand on a skull in the centre of the memorial. Physical death was more overtly represented in monuments in the later seventeenth century as part of the rise of Protestant secular imagery.

significant departure from the recumbent pose of earlier effigies and was probably intended to allow a superior level of interaction between statue and observer. Frequenters of the Minister could stare straight into the marble faces of Lord and Lady Strafford, and they in turn could gaze back. The upright postures of these and other monumental bodies, moreover, might enhance the posthumous authority of the aristocracy. William and Henrietta exude a confidence and majesty in standing that cannot be matched in effigies that are deferentially lying down.

The middling sort, if indeed they were lucky enough to secure an interior burial, brought simpler memorials through the doors of the parish church in this period. These were occasionally asked for in wills. William Fuller of Syleham, gentleman, willed in 1629 that his

31. A winged skull, part of the wall monument dedicated to Nathaniel and Jane Barnardiston, c.1660s.

32. The splendid white marble monument in York Minster commemorating William Wentworth, 2nd Earl of Strafford, and his first wife, Lady Henrietta. Henrietta died in 1685, while William joined her 10 years later at the age of 59, leaving no issue. The monument features two effigies standing up, allowing for a greater level of interaction between statue and observer. Between them rests a prominently positioned funeral urn.

executor see him buried near his late wife in the chancel of Syleham church, 'and…lay a decent stone or stones over our graves within one year of the day of my burial'. In 1620 the yeoman Reginald Burrough similarly instructed that, 'a gravestone is to be laid over [my] grave with a remembrance thereon who lies under it' in Bungay church. The 'practitioner in physic' Edmond Harris was extraordinarily specific about his memorial in Henstead church in 1622. Although its overall appearance was to be modest, its anticipated words were to be worth more than the riches of the aristocracy. Harris' executor was assigned the task of 'bestow[ing] on a gravestone of marble, six foot long and three foot broad' the following inscription:

> 'Hereunder resteth the body of Edmond Harris, gent., practitioner in physic, who deceased the -- day of -- in the year of our lord God 16--, & of his age --, & by his side rests the body of his (said) daughter Anne Harris who died the -- day of -- in the year 1---, & of her age'[6]

The epitaph was to read:

> 'Even suche a tyme that takes in trust, our youthe our Age and all we have, and paies us but with earth and dust, in darkesome night and silent grave, when we have wandered all our waies, and spent the Story of our daies, then from that grave of earth and dust, the Lorde will raise me uppe I trust'[7]

Both were to be engraved in brass. Harris' epitaph, a reproduction of Sir Walter Raleigh's final poem, indicates that he was submissively accepting of his fate as a mere corpse in a grave of 'earth and dust', silently awaiting the Resurrection. Perhaps this is precisely why he sought to include an inscription that acted as a reassuring remembrance of the living man and his daughter. The Harris example is an allusion to the post-Reformation desire in England for inscriptions to reflect more precisely the individualistic qualities of deceased persons.

No consideration of church memorials in seventeenth-century England would be complete without a mention of the royal monuments housed in Westminster Abbey. Elizabeth I's can be found residing in the north aisle of the Henry VII Chapel, where it was installed by her successor James I soon after her death in 1603, at a cost of £1,485. It is a beautiful monument of white marble, capturing the queen's regality even in her later years, but it would have been more striking when it was first constructed. The lions supporting the reclining effigy were originally gilded instead of pale, while certain features of the queen's apparel, including her robe, dress, and orb, may have been coloured. The tombs of two of James I's daughters were also erected in the north aisle of the Chapel and can be admired today along with Queen Elizabeth's monument. Both were made

33. A modest seventeenth-century gravestone set into the floor of Holy Trinity Church in Goodramgate, York, c.1689. The man buried beneath it had vague royal connections. The inscription reads: 'Here lyeth in hopes of a Blessed resurrection the body of Lyonel Elyott Youngest sonne of Tho: Elyott Groom of the bed Chamber to King Charles the 2(n)d who departed this life the 5(T)H March Anno Domini 1689'.

by the Flemish sculptor Maximilian Colt, who was likewise responsible for the effigy of the kingly Elizabeth a few years before. The monuments are all the more touching because both girls lived only very briefly. Sophia was three days old when she died in June 1606. She is depicted sleeping in a fine cradle adorned with an attractive gold pattern, beneath a dark coverlet trimmed with lace. Mary, aged two when she perished, is shown nearby in the classic recumbent position, resting an elbow on a pillow. Her tomb is extraordinarily lavish for one so young; cherubs sit at the base, the main body is lined with gold, and a lion sits at the princess's feet. The inscriptions appear to be attempts on the part of King James and Queen Anne to reconcile themselves to the loss of their small children. Sophia's reads:

'Sophia, a royal rosebud untimely plucked by Fate and from James, King of Great Britain, France and Ireland,

and Queen Anne her parents, snatched away, to flower again in the rose garden of Christ, lies here. 23rd June, 4th year of the reign of King James 1606.'

Mary's is no less heartrending:

'Mary, daughter of James King of Great Britain, France and Ireland and of Queen Anne; received into heaven in earliest infancy, I found joy for myself and left grief to my parents. 16th December 1607. Those who wish joy ask sympathy. She lived 2 years 5 months 8 days.'[8]

Not all members of the English royal family were blessed with such thoughtful commemorations. Constraints on space in the Henry VII Chapel meant that Charles II was given no monument at all after he died

34. The tomb effigy of Queen Elizabeth I in Westminster Abbey. The likeness of the monarch still reclines proud after 400 years of public display. The monument was commissioned by Elizabeth's successor, James I, and was intended to be a posthumous display of regality and queenly splendour. It is a white marble feature bordered by black pillars and now gold-topped railings, with lions supporting its base.

in 1685. A wax effigy of the king sat beside his grave for a hundred years instead. His niece, Mary II, faced the same problem in 1695, or rather her corpse did, which was appeased by the addition of a small stone to mark the spot where her body rested.

Moving now to the simplicities of the parish churchyard, those who were buried here might choose to be commemorated through the erection of a simple headstone. It was in the latter years of this century that headstones first began to be erected in English churchyards in significant numbers, in part due to the burgeoning desire from humbler men and women to be remembered in stone as their aristocratic counterparts were in churches. Designs remained mostly basic and devoid of eccentricity, echoing the status of the individual buried in the grave below. Chilham churchyard in Kent houses an excellent example of a seventeenth-century headstone dating from 1698. At its top is the amateurish image of a skull, the only decorative feature of the monument, while underneath lies a brief inscription detailing who is interred in the earth: Henry Knowler, husband of Frances and Ester Knowler. Within the grounds of St Mary's Church in Cheltenham can be found nestled a slightly more elaborate gravestone from 1679, belonging to a man called William. The stone is edged with a wavy border that comes together at the uppermost point to form a curling summit. Erosion through the years has left the exact pattern difficult to discern.

The distribution of remembrance objects was a practice observed by a considerable part of the population in seventeenth-century England. Since the sixteenth century rings of varying styles had been the most popular offering, but other remembrances might include anything from family plate to an old nag. The culture of gift-giving in this context rested on the principle that the object presented would remind the recipient of the person who had gifted it. The dead individual, whoever they might be, would therefore be remembered through the object. Thus, in 1634 Edward Baldry of Ipswich, yeoman, bequeathed in his will 40 shillings to his cousins Joan, Elizabeth, and Mary, to 'buy rings to wear as a remembrance of me'. A huge number of seventeenth-century wills include bequests of rings for this very purpose. The aristocratic testator, in particular, was keen to specify the type of remembrance ring he or she wished to bequeath to a beneficiary. Death's head rings were a firm favourite, being gold pieces that featured morbid depictions of heads or skulls in their centres. Edmund Pooley of Badley, esquire, set aside in 1607 certain 'sums' to be made into 'ringes with a Deaths head in remembrance of me', although he failed to name any beneficiaries. Pooley specified that his will had been written with his own hand. Dame Anne Wingfield of Letheringham bequeathed to each of her nephews and nieces 'a Deathes head Ringe of fortie shillings for a Remembrance' in 1625. More opulent types of remembrance ring were, likewise, given by high-ranking testators wishing to exhibit their status through bequests. Mary Cornwalleys of Ipswich, esquire's widow, bequeathed in her will of 1631 'one Diamonde Ringe of five poundes' to her 'deare and loving brother', desiring him to wear it 'in memory of her'. Dame Catherine Carey of Little Stonham, widow, bequeathed to her sister 'one Ringe of gould to be sett with 4 Diamonds made in the fashion of a harte of the price…of six Poundes thirteene shillings and foure pence'. Sir Ralph Verney sent a ring to his brother Henry on behalf of his deceased daughter Anna Maria in 1639. It contained a lock of the girl's hair. 'You shall herewithal receive a ring', Ralph wrote. He explained that, 'shee was fond of you, and you loved her, therefore I now send you this to keepe for her sake'.

There are examples of remembrance rings being used as bribes on occasion. Henry Beart of Hacheston, yeoman, bequeathed in 1624 a ring engraved with a death's head to 'friend' Henry Ewen, 'for his pains' in being a supervisor of the will. The bequest was seemingly made to assure Ewen that he would receive some form of payment, or

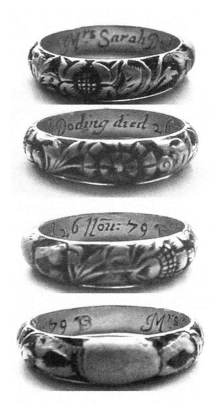

35. A seventeenth-century remembrance (or mourning) ring, seen from different angles, c.1679. It is a gold piece decorated with plants and a skull and crossbones on its outside. Inscribed in the middle are the words 'Mrs Sarah Doding died 26th Nov 79'. Mrs Doding was a resident of Lancashire. Rings were extremely popular in seventeenth-century England as a means by which to be remembered, often being designed with a death's head or skull.

151

recognition, were he to agree to the role. Thomas Goodwyn's will of 1635 provides a firmer example of this point. He willed the following:

> 'I doe make my especiall frendes Harbottle Wingfield Esquire and John Sheppard of Mendlesham gent. to be the Supervisors of this my will And doe give to each of them Tenn poundes apiece to buy them a piece of plate in remembrance of my love to them…hopeing that they wilbe assisting to my Executor'[9]

Goodwyn hoped that by bequeathing to his supervisors 'plate in remembrance of my love', it would encourage them to be 'assisting' to his executor.

Plate was given liberally as a remembrance by wealthy testators in the 1600s. Sometimes it was to be bought as opposed to coming directly from the family dresser. Mary Cornwalleys, esquire's widow, bequeathed a considerable £20 in 1631 to her cousin 'to buy him a piece of plate for a remembrance of me'. Sir Thomas Cambell aimed to be remembered by every member of the Ironmongers' Company in London in 1612 when he bequeathed to them £20 'to be ymployed in plate whereuppon I will have my name or Armes set'. Sir Humphrey Handford had the same idea 10 years later, in this case setting his sights on the Worshipful Company of Grocers, of which he was a member. In 1625 he willed:

> 'Item I give and bequeath unto the master wardens and cominalty of the arte or mistery of Grocers in London, whereof I am a member, for a remembrance of my love, soe much plate as shalbe worth thirty and three poundes six shillings and eight pence, the same plate to be made of such fashion with my name thereon as they shall appoint.'[10]

Money on its own was a popular remembrance gift too, with men bequeathing it more frequently than women. George Brome, gentleman, bequeathed to his 'Noble-friend and worthie Captaine' Sir Thomas Glemham, 'for a poore remembrance of my sincere affection and faithfull service towards him', £40 in 1627. Through this bequest, Brome wanted to be remembered to Glemham as an affectionate and faithful soldier, but also as a friend. Arthur Jenney of Knodishall, esquire, used a bequest of money to be remembered as a doting parent to his daughters, willing in 1604 that one of them should receive 'five poundes…in remembrance of my fatherly love and goodwill towardes them'.

Silver spoons were mentioned ubiquitously in wills, yet it seems that they were bequeathed to beneficiaries mainly on account of their monetary value. Husbandman Ralph Corbin of Weston, for instance, exemplifies the value placed on spoons in his will of 1622, mentioning that he had 'pawned 4 silver spoons to sister Cottman' for 20 shillings. Even though it is no great amount, that he pawned the spoons speaks volumes. However, Thomas Warde, a clothier from Needham Market, did bequeath his best silver spoons to his sons, daughter, and three grandchildren for 'a remembrance' in 1620.

The more unique remembrance gifts, found in isolation in a handful of wills, demonstrate that almost anything could be bequeathed as a 'remembrance' in early modern England. Alice Turner of Bungay, widow, desired in her will of 1622 that the 'gossip Thomas Francklin' receive 'for a remembrance [a] wrought table napkin' a month after her decease. The significance of such a bequest can never be known. Abrie Boteman of Badingham, spinster, bequeathed in her will of 1625 'a new piece of lawn' (a kind of fine linen) to Anne Lyngwood 'for a small remembrance'. At least two testators bequeathed desks. One of them, Stephen Rose of Wickham Market, yeoman, bequeathed to his son-in-law a 'desk standing in the parlour chamber & a book', both specifically termed 'remembrances'. Lady Anne Clifford's instructions in 1674 were undeniably exceptional. She wrote:

> 'To my right honorable and noble grandsonne, Nicholas Earle of Thanett, one other gold cupp with a cover to itt, all of massie gold, which cost me alsoe about 100l., whereon the armes of his father, my deceased son-in-law, and of his mother, my daughter, and some of my owne armes, are engraven, desiring his lordshipp that the same remaine after his decease (if he soe please) to his wife, my honorable cossen and goddaughter, if she survive him, as a remembrance of me.'

Anne also wanted her father, George Clifford, to be remembered through a peculiarly aristocratic bequest:

> 'To my honorable grandchildren, Nicholas Earle of Thanett and Mr. John Tufton, his brother, the remainder of the two

rich armors which were my noble father's, to remaine to them and their posterity (if they soe please) as a remembrance of him.'[11]

Ralph Josselin's wife was given the customary ring to remember their friend Mrs Mary by in 1647. Ralph himself, much more bizarrely, was left a 'silver tooth and eare pick'.

Horses were bequeathed to beneficiaries as remembrances on several different occasions in seventeenth-century Suffolk. On one occasion in 1627, George Brome bequeathed to his brother 'my nagge as a remembrance of my love to him'. Thomas Roe of Walton, gentleman, gave to John Scrutton 'the bay nag I usually ride in token of the old affection which was always between us' in 1634. The horse was clearly given as a 'remembrance' – in all but name – of the ties of affection between the two men. The latter two examples are suggestive of a pervasive desire to use remembrance bequests as a way of recalling and reinforcing testators' ties of affection, and thus their earthly connections, after death. Members of the gentry stipulated that bequests be remembrances of ties of affection across the period. Edward Bacon of Barham, esquire, bequeathed in 1613 to his 'most lovinge and deare Sister…to whome I have been bound above all others a Ryng of twentie shillinges as a token of my last love'. Mary Cornwalleys of Ipswich, esquire's widow, willed the following in 1631:

> 'Item I give to my worthy aproved loveinge and kinde Nephew Mr John [Prishon?]…my Ringe with five Diamonds, the pledge of love betwixt my deare husband and me, which I desire him to weare for my sake.'[12]

This example is interesting because the bequest is seemingly used as an intended remembrance of the ties of affection between the testator and her husband, even though the beneficiary was Cornwalleys' nephew. A thought-provoking observation is the desire in wills for ties of affection to be recollected posthumously between masters and their servants. Sir William Cornwallis of Brome, knight, bequeathed in his will of 1611 £10 apiece to his servants 'for a remembrance of my love and good will towards them'. George Brome, as a kind of subservient figure, bequeathed many gifts to the Glemham family in remembrance of the 'love', 'affection', and 'observance' he showed them all in life. The Glemhams prospered under the Tudors, being by the early seventeenth century a well-established family based at Glemham Hall on the outskirts of Little Glemham, on the Suffolk coast. Gift exchange in these instances was probably the consequence of a paternalistic association. This is no doubt true of Sir William Cornwallis' kindly bequest to his servants.

A prominent and meticulous remembrance bequest appears in the 1637 will of Sir Francis Nedham of Barking Hall. He willed:

> '…my Executors to bestowe six poundes thirteene shillings [4] pence upon a faire communion Cup…of twentie ounces of silver…to remayne for a Remembrance of mee to the parish of Barking. About the brimme whereof on the outside to be engraven in greate Romane letters *Quid retribuam Domino pro omnibus quæ retribuit mihi*. And about the middle or body of the said Cupp to be written in like Romane…but of a lesser size *Accipiam calicem salutaris, et agam Domino gratias reddam*; And at the bottome of the Cupp in like letters as those in the midst *Ex dono Francisei Nedham militis*. & the day of the month when it was made'[13]

The communion cup, which would most likely be kept in Barking parish church, was gifted to the entire parish. Through it, every member of Barking was expected to remember the great Sir Francis Nedham. The words to go about the brim of the cup, *Quid retribuam Domino pro omnibus quæ retribuit mihi*, roughly translate as, 'What shall I render to the Lord, for all the things he hath rendered unto me?'. Those destined to be etched about the middle of the cup, *Accipiam calicem salutaris, et agam Domino gratias reddam*, more or less translate as, 'I will take the cup of salvation, and my Lord, I thank you', while *Ex dono Francisei Nedham militis* translates as, 'a gift from Francis Nedham, soldier'. On the one hand, it seems Nedham wished to be remembered to the parish within a godly context, having bequeathed a communion cup emblazoned with the traditional language of the Church: Latin. This was also a language out of reach of most of the population in early seventeenth-century England, and so it may have placed further emphasis on his esteemed membership of the literate class. That the communion cup was intended for widespread commemoration of Nedham within the focal point of the parish, the church, makes it likely that his ultimate desire was to be remembered as a man of prominence and influence within Barking. It was a further way in which the deferential relationship between the parish and its resident aristocrat(s) could be upheld after the latter's demise.

In August 1670 Giles Moore highlighted the seemingly obligatory nature of remembrances when he touched on his brother's will in his diary. In the first draft of the will, Moore grumbled, 'there was nothing at all given to any of his kindred, nor the least mention made of them'. Moore confronted his brother about the omission after he had made sure that the room in which he lay dying was empty. Evidently it was a sensitive issue that required a hushed, but equally animated, discussion. The vicar relayed to his sibling that, while he himself did not 'desyre or expect anything from him', his other poorer kindred might. 'If hee left them nothing at all for a remembrance, they would bee apt to thinke that hee had quite forgot them', Moore concluded. Ralph Josselin felt quite forgotten in 1680 when Lady Honywood died and left him nothing to remember her by in her will. Josselin complained that they had known each other for 40 years, during which time he had been 'serviceable every way to her for soule & body, and in her estate more then ordinery'. He seemed to believe that this entitled him to some form of 'legacy', a legacy that upon her death was not delivered.

Wills do not tell us when remembrances were actually given to individuals in this century, or if indeed they were given to the intended beneficiaries at all. Evidence suggests that they were sometimes handed out on the day of a person's funeral, often doubling up as mourning accessories to be worn as a mark of respect. At the funeral of John Evelyn's son Richard in 1658, rings were distributed to the mourners present with the motto *Dominus abstulit* ('the Lord takes away') engraved on them. Samuel Pepys had 'wine and rings' at the burial of Mr Russell in January 1663, surrounded by a 'great and good company of aldermen'. Ralph Josselin targeted Lady Honywood's funeral as part of his continued ill feeling towards her in 1680, commenting afterwards:

> 'Not a glove, ribband, scutcheon, wine, beare, bisquett given
> at her burial but a litle mourning to servants.'[14]

Ralph had been unlucky. In the opening years of the eighteenth century the practice experienced by Evelyn and Pepys was as popular as ever in England, if not a little excessively executed at times. Dr Thomas Gale, who had been the Dean of York since 1697, was interred with 'great solemnity' in York in 1702, which included the distribution of 200 rings, gloves 'for all', and scarves for the bearers of his coffin. Ralph Thoresby recollected that he received his ring in a room that was so crowded it 'could not contain the company'.

The deathbed, or the final moments before death, also saw the physical giving of remembrances in seventeenth-century England, as has already been observed. In 1635 Eleanor Evelyn gave her children rings from the deathbed, and so too Charles I, mere hours away from his execution, provided his royal offspring with rings to remember their father by. Such offerings were undoubtedly more concerned with the keeping alive of a person's memory, or the ties of affection between individuals, than those objects that were distributed in large quantities at burials.

Conclusion

The Seventeenth Century and Beyond

In 2002, at the age of 71, Queen Elizabeth II's younger sister, Princess Margaret, died after years of ill health at King Edward VII's Hospital in London. In line with her wishes the subsequent funeral was a simple one. A mere 450 mourners attended the service at St George's Chapel on 15 February. The previous night Margaret's coffined body had been kept in solitude in the nave, and around an hour before the funeral was due to start it was carried to the choir by a handful of servicemen from her regiment. A small band of royalist well-wishers had turned up at Windsor to bid farewell to the princess, but they would not have seen much of the day's events. It was regarded as a private affair, meaning that there was no expectation for the general public to play an active role in Margaret's funeral solemnities. Accordingly, cameras were not permitted to enter the Chapel to film the service.

Whether the princess knew it or not, hers was a type of royal funeral that could be traced back to the days of Restoration England. In 1685 Charles II set the trend for private funerals of prominent members of the English royal family when he was interred in Westminster Abbey at nighttime. As we have already seen, unlike his regal seventeenth-century contemporaries, the king was buried with very little pomp on 14 February. The funeral attracted comment for its bewildering simplicity. Samuel Newton wrote afterwards from Cambridge that the king had been interred, 'in a very hansome and decent order as could bee for a private Funerall'. So too in 2002, *The Guardian* reported that it had been a 'quiet funeral' for Princess Margaret, 'far removed from Princess Diana's funeral' five years earlier in September 1997.

Seventeenth-century England was a trendsetter for many rituals associated with death that would continue into the eighteenth century and beyond. It had seen the rise of the secular deathbed scene, the introduction of the coffin as a standard feature of the disposal of the dead, and the intensification of memorials that placed emphasis on individualistic qualities, including graves in churchyards. Most significantly of all it had witnessed the birth of the undertaking trade. By the mid-1700s this trade was in full swing. The 1752 trade card of the coffin dealer and undertaker Robert Green, based in St Margaret's Hill, Southwark, shows how far the undertaking business had come in only a short space of time. The card announced that Green sold and let 'all manner of furniture for funerals, on reasonable terms'. This included:

> 'Velvet Palls, Hangings for Rooms, large Silver'd Candlesticks & Sconces, Tapers & Wax Lights, Heraldry, Feathers & Velvets, fine Cloth Cloaks…Silk Scarves, Allamode & Sarsnett Hatbands, Italian Crape by the Piece or Hatband, black & white favours, Cloth Black, or Grey: Bays & Flannel…Burying Crapes of all sorts, fine Quilting & Quilted Mattrices the best Lac'd, Plain & Shammy Gloves, Kidd & Lamb…All sorts of Plates & Handles for Coffins in Brass, Lead or Tin, likewise Nails of all sorts, Coffins & Shrouds of all sizes ready made.'[1]

Green had all bases covered, providing everything from fine cloth cloaks, silk scarves, and sarsenet hatbands to nails for the coffin. From approximately 1800 onwards the trade had come to dominate English funerals to such an extent that some commentators wrote about undertakers unfavourably, believing them to be a law unto themselves. In around 1811 the essayist Charles Lamb made the following flinty remarks about the professionals who dealt with death:

> 'He is a master of the ceremonies at burials and mourning assemblies, grand marshal at funeral processions, the only true yeoman of the body, over which he exercises a dictatorial authority from the moment that the breath has taken leave to

159

that of its final commitment to the earth. His ministry begins where the physician's, the lawyer's, and the divine's, end. [...] His temporalities remain unquestioned. He is arbitrator of all questions of honour which may concern the defunct; and upon slight inspection will pronounce how long he may remain in this upper world with credit to himself, and when it will be prudent for his reputation that he should retire.'[2]

Unfortunately for Lamb, the trade and its tradesmen were here to stay. A century later in 1935, a few years before the outbreak of the Second World War, the British Undertakers Association took over the organisation of funerals completely and unequivocally in collectively rebranding itself as the National Association of Funeral Directors. Along with providing funeral furnishings and transport for the body, undertakers now also offered spaces in which to store the corpse prior to the day of the funeral, including chapels of rest. The biggest development in their services, however, was the introduction of the option of cremation.

As well as continuing the death practices of the seventeenth century, the decades and centuries after the 1600s similarly experienced palpable changes in this sphere. Nineteenth-century England spawned an interesting mix of the old and the new. The newfound and macabre obsession with dying for which the Victorians have become infamous was a reality only up to a certain point. It is true that some funerals were outlandishly extravagant in the 1800s, the likes of which would have been quite alien to those living in the country 200 years before, even if such individuals had been a party to a seventeenth-century royal ceremony or two. The Duke of Wellington's funeral in 1852 was unlike anything ever seen before in England. The pageantry was matchless, the scale overwhelming. *The London Illustrated News* reported on 27 November:

> 'No one can hope worthily to describe the splendour, magnificence, and solemnity of that great state pageant, or the imposing interest which it derived from the countless thousands of human beings who swarmed along the line of [the] route and reverently stood with uncovered heads as the bier of the venerated dead passed before them. England's metropolis – vast, populous, mighty London – empress of

modern cities – the huge living wonder of the nineteenth century – never before presented a scene so amazing to men of other lands or even to her own sons.'[3]

One of the more insalubrious outcomes of the Victorian thirst for death, or the thirst for the enhanced acknowledgment of death, was the advent of the photographed corpse. As photography developed in the middle of the century and reached out to a wider market, there grew an intriguing desire for posthumous images to be captured of deceased loved ones, often propped up in chairs or against people to give the impression that they were still alive. Sometimes eyes were painted on after the photograph had been taken to add to the sense of livingness. Such eccentric behaviour could find no tangible roots in the seventeenth century, although the desire to commemorate had clearly stood the test of time.

At the same time, the Victorian outlook on death was not so different from that of Stuart England. Wellington's funeral was a one-off spectacle, designed to evoke feelings of adulation and wonder. The majority of prominent Victorian men favoured minimalism over ostentation, mirroring a taste for private funerals developed in the seventeenth century by their titled forebears. Prime Minister William Gladstone offered a public funeral at Westminster Abbey following the death of the Earl of Beaconsfield, his predecessor, in 1881, but it was rejected. Benjamin Disraeli (the said earl) had requested in his will that he be honoured with a modest interment in the churchyard at Hughenden, Buckinghamshire, in the vault where his wife already lay. His wishes were duly carried out. The same occurrence was to be witnessed the following year in the wake of the death of Archbishop Archibald Campbell Tait. Considering his public and particularly his religious standing, many, including Queen Victoria, thought it appropriate that he be given a funeral and grave in Westminster Abbey. Tait's family argued that he had always expected a simpler send-off at Addington church, near to Addington Palace, the Archbishop of Canterbury's official residence in the nineteenth century. There he had erected a simple cross beneath which rested the bodies of his wife and son. The queen was persuaded that the wishes of Tait and his family should be respected. In contrast to Tait's private funeral, ornate monuments were commissioned for erection in Canterbury Cathedral, Westminster Abbey, and Rugby School Chapel.

The causes of death in England altered radically after the seventeenth century. While the reigns of terror of certain diseases, such as smallpox, continued for generations afterwards, others virtually disappeared. Major outbreaks of plague ceased to exist in the country after 1665, and in 1679 the last ever reported case of the disease in London was recorded. Appalling insanitary conditions in towns and cities led to new epidemics taking the place of the old. Cholera arrived in England in October 1831 and was in London by February 1832, resulting in an initial epidemic that crippled the capital and took the lives of between 4,000 and 7,000 citizens. Another serious outbreak occurred in 1854 in the Soho district of the City of Westminster, made famous because it was during this visitation that the physician John Snow came to the conclusion that cholera originated from contaminated water. It did not leave the city alone until the 1860s. The suffering caused by cholera was acute, making for a painful death that could be drawn out over several days. The first recorded case in Durham was reported in minute detail in the *Cholera Gazette* on 28 January 1832, by a surgeon called Balfour. The patient was a 67-year-old workhouse inmate, Matthew Ingram. Balfour found the man 'seated in a chair apparently inanimate', in a state of 'perfect asphyxia, the pulse imperceptible, face cold and pallid, eyes closed, and the mouth wide open'. He continued:

'Upon making enquiry respecting the cause and continuance of the patient's alarming condition, I learnt that he had been harassed by a severe purging since two o'clock; cramps had preceded the discharge, and were very severe, his feet were cold, and his fingers of a blue colour. I immediately assisted in having him removed from the fireside to his bed; and whilst carrying him along the room, there took place an involuntary alvine discharge of a stream of pale-coloured fluid. A small quantity of brandy and mint water, with 25 drops of laudanum, was administered; a bottle of hot water was applied to his feet, and he was closely enveloped with heated blankets. In the course of a few minutes, animation became more evident, he raised his eyelids and moved his limbs; soon after he was able to speak in a low tone of voice, and complained of cramps in his hands and feet.'

That was 10.00am on 7 January. The next day, at 10.00am again, Ingram's condition seemed to have stabilised. The vomiting had abated and his cramps were 'less severe', although his voice was weaker and he had developed sunken eyes 'surrounded by a dark areola'. By 2.00pm, however, Ingram's disorder appeared hopeless. Balfour recollected:

'Found the patient comatose, and sinking rapidly.'[4]

An hour later Ingram was dead.

In the early twentieth century it was an airborne virus, not one found in dirty water, that brought the country to its knees. The Spanish flu pandemic killed over half a million people in England over 1918-19, often very quickly and with little warning. Some victims developed pneumonia, turned blue, and suffocated to death just a few hours after presenting with the initial symptoms of a fever and headache.

Death by capital punishment continued into the twentieth century, although its application decreased decidedly during the eighteenth and nineteenth centuries. It was in the 1800s that the death knell was truly sounded for this divisive sentence. A string of events undermined the practice after 1800, beginning with the legal reformer Sir Samuel Romilly's crusade against capital punishment in the initial years of the century. He was not alone in his convictions. Shortly before his death in 1818, Romilly noted the comments of his fellow reformer Elizabeth Fry:

'She told me that there prevails among them [prisoners] a very strong and general sense of the great injustice of punishing mere thefts and forgeries in the same manner as murders; that it is frequently said by them, that the crimes of which they have been guilty are nothing, when compared with the crimes of Government towards themselves; that they have only been thieves, but that their governors are murderers.'[5]

In 1800 there were some 200 capital offences in existence in England. By 1840, following a major overhaul of the penal system, this number had been reduced to just seven. By 1861 it had dropped to four. The 1860s saw a forceful attack launched on the various punishments themselves. In 1868 public hangings were stopped for good. Hanging, drawing, and quartering, so popular in the seventeenth century, was abolished in 1870, having not been used for 50 years. At this point in English history the most common form of punishment had become imprisonment. Capital punishment was abolished for the crime of murder, and therefore outlawed more or less completely, 100 years later in 1965. The last felons to face the hangman's noose in the country were Peter Anthony Allen and Gwynne Owen Evans, both of whom were condemned for the murder of a 53-year-old van driver. They were put to death at Manchester and Liverpool on 13 August 1964.

To return to the point made at the beginning of this conclusion, however, we can be quite certain that the culture of death in seventeenth-century England left, and continues to leave, a lasting mark on successive eras. One of its greatest legacies is the determination to combat the oblivion of dying with the reinforcement of earthly connections. Wills were especially evocative of this blossoming attitude, which is why such emphasis has been placed on them in the preceding pages of this book.

Now ending where we began, the pervasive nature of death in seventeenth-century England is reiterated by the enigmatically named 'H.W.' in *The House of Mourning*, printed in 1640:

> '*It is appointed for all men once to die* […] There is no Age, Estate, Condition or ranke of men, but have beene foyled with that invincible Champion death; who riding up and downe the world upon his pale Horse above these five thousand yeares, hath with an impartiall stroke laid all flat before him: some in their Infancie have proved what it is to die before they knew what it was to live; others in the strength of Youth; some in their Old Age: rich and poore, high and low, of all sorts; young men may die, old men must die […] *What man is he that liveth and shall not see death?*'[6]

Chapter Notes

Introduction

1. Thomas Taylor Lewis (ed.), *Letters of the Lady Brilliana Harley* (London: Camden Society, 1854), pp. 246–7.
2. Randolph Yearwood, *The Penitent Murderer. Being An Exact Narrative Of the Life and Death of Nathaniel Butler* (London: T. Newcomb, 1659), pp. 25–6.
3. Ibid., p.26.

Chapter One: The Natural Death

1. E. Hockliffe (ed.), *The Diary of the Rev. Ralph Josselin*, Camden Third Series, Vol. 15 (London: Royal Historical Society, 1908), p.74.
2. Anthony Walker (ed.), *Memoir of Lady Warwick: Also Her Diary* (London: The Religious Tract Society, 1847), p.111.
3. Henry Ellis (ed.), *Original Letters Illustrative of English History*, Second Series, Vol. 4 (London: Harding and Lepard, 1827), p.37.
4. William Bray (ed.), *The Diary of John Evelyn*, Vol. 1 (London: J.M. Dent & Sons Ltd, 1907), p.404.
5. Margaret M. Verney (ed.), *Memoirs of the Verney Family*, Vol. 2 (London: Longmans, Green, and Co., 1904), p.250.
6. S. Wilton Rix (ed.), *The Diary and Autobiography of Edmund Bohun Esq.* (Beccles: Read Crisp, 1853), p.38.
7. Ibid., pp. 38–9.

8. Andrew Clark (ed.), *The Life and Times of Anthony Wood*, Vol. 2, Oxford Historical Society, Vol. 21 (Oxford: Clarendon Press, 1892), p.101.
9. Anon. (ed.), *William Lilly's History of His Life and Times* (London: Charles Baldwyn, 1822), p.30.
10. Thomas Heywood (ed.), *The Diary of the Rev. Henry Newcome*, The Chetham Society, Vol. 18 (Manchester: The Chetham Society, 1849), p.15.

Chapter Two: The Soldierly Death

1. Francis Gregory, *A thanksgiving sermon for peace abroad* (London: Richard Sare, 1697), p.13.
2. C.H. Firth (ed.), *The Memoirs of Edmund Ludlow* (Oxford: Clarendon Press, 1894), p.103.
3. G. Roberts, *The History of Lyme-Regis, Dorset, From the Earliest Periods to the Present Day* (Sherborne: Langdon and Harker, 1823), p.46.
4. William Douglas Hamilton (ed.), *Calendar of State Papers, Domestic Series, of the Reign of Charles I, 1644–1645* (London: Eyre and Spottiswoode, 1890), p.45.
5. Henry B. Wheatley (ed.), *The Diary of Samuel Pepys*, Vol. 1 (New York: Random House, pref. 1893), pp. 1098–9.
6. 'Cornelis Tromp' appears to be the standard form of his name, as opposed to Cornelius van Tromp.
7. Anon., *The life of Cornelius Van Tromp, Lieutenant-Admiral of Holland and Westfriesland* (London: J. Orme, 1697), p.449.
8. Daniel Defoe, *Curious and diverting journies, thro' the whole island of Great-Britain* (London: G. Parker, 1734), no page number given.
9. Edward Maunde Thompson (ed.), *Correspondence of the Family of Hatton*, Vol. 2 (London: The Camden Society, 1878), pp. 99–100.

Chapter Three: The Criminal Death

1. Norman Egbert McClure (ed.), *The Letters of John Chamberlain*, Vol. 2 (Philadelphia: The American Philosophical Society, 1939), p.15.
2. Mary Anne Everett Green (ed.), *Diary of John Rous* (London: The Camden Society, 1856), pp. 30–1.
3. J.C. Hodgson (ed.), *Six North Country Diaries*, Surtrees Society, Vol. 118 (Durham: Andrews and Co., 1910), p.46.

4. McClure, *The Letters of John Chamberlain*, Vol. 1, pp. 297–8.
5. Anon. (ed.), *A Brief Historical Relation of State Affairs from September 1678 to April 1714 (Narcissus Luttrell)*, Vol. 4 (Oxford: Oxford University Press, 1847), p.418.
6. Maunde Thompson, *Correspondence of the Family of Hatton*, Vol. 1, p.131.
7. Anon. (ed.), *Murder and Petty-Treason: or, Bloody News from Southwark* (London, 1677), p.7.
8. Andrew Clark (ed.), *The Life and Times of Anthony Wood*, Vol. 3, Oxford Historical Society, Vol. 26 (Oxford: Clarendon Press, 1894), pp. 552–3.
9. George Roberts, *The Life, Progresses, and Rebellion of James, Duke of Monmouth*, Vol. 2 (London: Longman, Brown, Green, and Longmans, 1844), pp. 224–5.
10. Anon., *The last words of Coll. Richard Rumbold, Mad. Alicia Lisle, Alderman Henry Cornish, and Mr.Richard Nelthrop who were executed in England and Scotland for high treason in the year 1685* (London, 1685), pp. 3–4.
11. Verney, *Memoirs*, Vol. 2, pp. 404–5.
12. Anon., *England's Black Tribunal Containing: I. The Complete Tryal of King Charles the First (...)* (London: R. Freeman, 1747), pp. 5–6.

Chapter Four: The Deathbed

1. J.B. Williams, *Memoirs of the Life, Character, and Writings of the Rev. Matthew Henry* (London: J. Holdsworth, 1828), p.256.
2. Wheatley, *Pepys*, Vol. 1, p.859.
3. Anon. (ed.), *Historical Notices of Events Occurring Chiefly in the Reign of Charles I (Nehemiah Wallington)*, Vol. 1 (London: Richard Bentley, 1869), p.197.
4. The will of Sir John Croftes, 1 Feb 1630, PCCRP: Will Registers PROB 11/157/102. (1 Feb 1630 was the date of probate.)

Chapter Five: Of Corpses, Coffins, and Carriages

1. Linda A. Pollock, *With Faith and Physic: The Life of a Tudor Gentlewoman, Lady Grace Mildmay, 1552–1620* (London: Collins & Brown, 1993), p.40.

2. Charles Severn (ed.), *Diary of the Rev. John Ward* (London: Henry Colburn, 1839), p.261.
3. Ellis, *Original Letters*, Vol. 4, p.37.
4. M. Misson, *Memoirs and Observations in His Travels Over England* (London, 1719), pp. 89–90.
5. J.E. Foster (ed.), *The Diary of Samuel Newton* (Cambridge: Cambridge Antiquarian Society, 1890), pp. 18–9.
6. Various (eds), *Transactions of the Royal Historical Society*, New Series, Vol. 6 (London: Longmans, Green, and Co., 1892), p.7.
7. The will of Sir Thomas Cornwallis, 6 Feb 1605, PCCRP: Will Registers PROB 11/105/106.
8. Verney, *Memoirs*, Vol. 2, p.417.

Chapter Six: The Common and the Noble Funeral

1. John Dunton, *A Mourning-Ring in memory of your departed Friend* (London, 1692), p.289.
2. Elizabeth Cust (ed.), *Records of the Cust Family, Series II: The Brownlows of Belton, 1550–1779* (London: Mitchell Hughes and Clarke, 1909), pp. 173–4.
3. The will of Sir Thomas Cambell, 12 March 1614, PCCRP: Will Registers PROB 11/123/273.
4. The will of Alexander Eylmer, 13 Aug 1602, PCCRP: Will Registers PROB 11/100/144.
5. Thomas Ken, *A sermon preached at the funeral of the Right Honourable the Lady Margaret Mainard, at Little Easton in Essex, on the 30th of June, 1682* (London, 1688), no page number given.
6. Matthew Henry Lee (ed.), *Diaries and Letters of Philip Henry* (London: Kegan Paul, Trench & Co., 1882), p.116.
7. Henry James Morehouse (ed.), *Extracts from the Diary of the Rev. Robert Meeke* (London: H.G. Bohn, 1874), p.50.
8. J. Horsfall Turner (ed.), *The Rev. Oliver Heywood: His Autobiography, Diaries, Anecdote and Event Books*, Vol. 1 (Brighouse: 1882), p.339.
9. Various (eds), *Transactions of the Essex Archaeological Society,* Vol. 1 (Colchester: The Essex and West Suffolk Gazette Office, 1858), p.119.
10. Various, *Transactions of the Essex Archaeological Society*, Vol. 1, p.118.

11. James Orchard Halliwell (ed.), *The Autobiography and Correspondence of Sir Simonds d'Ewes*, Vol. 1 (London: Richard Bentley, 1845), p.132.
12. Verney, *Memoirs*, Vol. 2, p.501.

Chapter Seven: Royal Funerals

1. Walter Scott (ed.), *A Collection of Scarce and Valuable Tracts*, Vol. 1 (London: anonymous printer, 1809), p.250.
2. James Heath, *Flagellum: or the Life and Death, Birth and Burial of O. Cromwell* (London, 1665), pp. 195–6.
3. Bray, *Evelyn*, Vol. 2, p.336.

Chapter Eight: The Unorthodox Burial

1. Harry Gill and Everard L. Guilford (eds), *The Rector's Book (William Sampson)* (Nottingham: H.B. Saxton, 1910), p.63.
2. J. Charles Cox, *The Parish Registers of England* (London: Methuen & Co. Ltd, 1910), p.175.
3. Foster, *Newton*, p.109.
4. Wheatley, *Pepys*, Vol. 2, p.38.
5. Anon., *Historical Notices*, Vol. 2, p.134.
6. Thomas Ellison Gibson (ed.), *Crosby Records: A Chapter of Lancashire Recusancy*, The Chetham Society, Vol. 12 (Manchester: Charles E. Simms, 1887), p.42.
7. Ellison Gibson, *Crosby Records*, p.45.
8. William Warburton (ed.), *The History of the Rebellion and Civil Wars in England (Clarendon)*, Vol. 7 (Oxford: Clarendon Press, 1826), p.290.
9. Everett Green, *John Rous*, p.76.
10. Heywood, *Henry Newcome*, p.73.

Chapter Nine: Remembrance

1. John Clay (ed.), *North Country Wills, 1383–1558*, Surtrees Society, Vol. 116 (Durham: Andrews & Co., 1908), p.51.
2. The will of Sir William Cornwallis, 27 Nov 1611, PCCRP: Will Registers PROB 11/118/441.

3. John Blatchly, "The lost and mutilated memorials of the Bovile and Wingfield families at Letheringham," in *Proceedings of the Suffolk Institute for Archaeology and History* 33, No. 2 (1974), p.190.
4. Catherine E. Parsons, *All Saints' Church Horseheath* (Cambridge: Cambridge University Press, 1911), p.47.
5. Verney, *Memoirs*, Vol. 1, p.530.
6. Will no. 245 in Marion E. Allen (ed.), *Wills of the Archdeaconry of Suffolk, 1620–1624* (Woodbridge: The Boydell Press, 1989), p.137.
7. IC/AA1, Wills, Suffolk Records Office, Ipswich.
8. As seen on the monuments in Westminster Abbey.
9. The will of Thomas Goodwyn, 25 Apr 1638, PCCRP: Will Registers PROB 11/176/543.
10. The will of Sir Humphrey Handford, 8 Dec 1625, PCCRP: Will Registers PROB 11/147/493.
11. George C. Williamson (ed.), *Lady Anne Clifford, Countess of Dorset, Pembroke & Montgomery, 1590–1676: Her Life, Letters, and Work* (Kendal: Titus Wilson and Son, 1922), p.467.
12. The will of Mary Cornwalleys, 29 Feb 1632, PCCRP: Will Registers PROB 11/161/282.
13. The will of Sir Francis Nedham, 11 May 1638, PCCRP: Will Registers PROB 11/177/96.
14. Hockliffe, *Josselin*, p.179.

Conclusion: The Seventeenth Century and Beyond

1. Words from the trade card of the undertaker and coffin dealer Robert Green (London, 1752).
2. Thomas Noon Talfourd (ed.), *The Works of Charles Lamb* (London: Edward Moxon, 1848), p.63.
3. Anon., "The Grand State Funeral of Arthur Duke of Wellington," *The Illustrated London News*, 27 Nov 1852, p.17.
4. Anon., *The Cholera Gazette, Consisting of Documents Communicated by the Central Board of Health* (London: S. Highley, 1832), pp. 37–8.
5. Romillys (eds), *The Life of Sir Samuel Romilly*, Vol. 2 (London: John Murray, 1842), pp. 486–7.
6. H.W., *The House of Mourning* (London, 1640), no page number given.

Bibliography

Primary Sources

Wills

The wills of the aristocracy were mainly found in:

Prerogative Court of Canterbury and Related Probate Jurisdictions, Will Registers, PROB 11, The National Archives, Kew, London

The wills of the middling sort were mainly found in:

IC/AA1, Wills, Suffolk Records Office, Ipswich
Allen, Marion E. (ed.), *Wills of the Archdeaconry of Suffolk, 1620–1624* (Woodbridge: The Boydell Press, 1989)
Allen, Marion E. (ed.), *Wills of the Archdeaconry of Suffolk, 1625–1626* (Woodbridge: The Boydell Press, 1995)
Allen, Marion E. (ed.), *Wills of the Archdeaconry of Suffolk, 1627–1628* (Woodbridge: The Boydell Press, 2015)
Allen, Marion E. and Nesta R. Evans (eds), *Wills from the Archdeaconry of Suffolk, 1629–1636* (Boston: New England Historic Genealogical Society, 1986)
Clay, John (ed.), *North Country Wills, 1383–1558*, Surtrees Society, Vol. 116 (Durham: Andrews & Co., 1908)

Gray, George J. and William Mortlock Palmer (eds), *Abstracts from the Wills and Testamentary Documents of Printers, Binders, and Stationers of Cambridge, 1504–1699* (London: Blades, East & Blades, 1915)

Siraut, Mary (ed.), *Somerset Wills*, Somerset Record Society, Vol. 89 (Bristol: J.W. Arrowsmith Ltd., 2003)

Quarter Sessions and Assize Records

Allen, D.H. (ed.), *Essex Quarter Sessions Order Book, 1652-1661* (Ipswich: W.S. Cowell Ltd., 1974)

Bates Harbin, E.H. (ed.), *Quarter Sessions Records for the County of Somerset, Volume 3: Commonwealth, 1646-1660* (London: Harrison and Sons Ltd., 1912)

Cockburn, J.S. (ed.), *Calendar of Assize Records: Kent Indictments, Charles II, 1676–1688*, Calendar Assize Records Series, Vol. 6 (Woodbridge: The Boydell Press, 1997)

Hardy, William Le (ed.), *County of Buckinghamshire, Calendar to the Sessions Records: Volume 1, 1678-1694* (Aylesbury: Hunt, Barnard & Co. Ltd., 1933)

Ratcliff, S.C. and H.C. Johnson (eds), *Warwick County Records, Volume 3: Quarter Sessions Order Book, Easter 1650 to Epiphany 1657* (Kettering: The Northamptonshire Printing and Publishing Company Ltd., 1937)

"Petitions," *Civil War Petitions: Conflict, Welfare, and Memory during and after the English Civil Wars, 1642–1710*, https://www.civilwarpetitions.ac.uk/

Parish Burial Registers

Beilby Cook, Robert (ed.), *The Parish Registers of St Martin, Coney Street, York, 1557–1812*, The Yorkshire Parish Register Society, Vol. 36 (Leeds: Oriel Press, 1909)

Brooke, J.M.S. and A.W.C. Hallen (eds), *The Transcript of the Registers of the United Parishes of St Mary Woolnoth and St Mary Woolchurch Haw, in the City of London, 1538– 1760* (London: Bowles & Sons, 1886)

Chester, Joseph Lemuel (ed.), *The Parish Registers of St Michael, Cornhill, London, 1546–1754*, The Harleian Society, Vol. 7 (London: The Harleian Society, 1882)

Collins, Francis (ed.), *The Registers of St Michael le Belfrey, York, Part II: Marriages, 1653–1772, Baptisms and Burials, 1653–1778*, The Yorkshire Parish Register Society, Vol. 11 (Leeds: Knight and Forster, 1901)

Cookson, Edward (ed.), *The Registers of St Nicholas, Ipswich, 1539–1710*, The Parish Register Society, Vol. 7 (London: anonymous printer, 1897)

Cox, J. Charles, *The Parish Registers of England* (London: Methuen & Co. Ltd, 1910)

Horsfall Turner, J. (ed.), *The Nonconformist Register, Of Baptisms, Marriages, and Deaths, Compiled by the Revs Oliver Heywood & T. Dickenson* (Brighouse: J.S. Jowett, 1881)

Diaries, Memoirs, Papers, Broadsheets, Sermons etc.

Anon., *A generall Bill for this present year, ending the 19 of December 1665* (London: 1665)

Anon., *Rules and Orders To be observed by all Justices of Peace, Mayors, Bayliffs, and other Officers, for prevention of the spreading of the Infection of the Plague* (London: John Bill and Christopher Barker, 1666)

Anon. (ed.), *William Whiteway of Dorchester: His Diary, 1618–1635*, Dorset Record Society, Vol. 12 (Dorchester: Dorset Record Society, 2015)

Anon. (ed.), *William Lilly's History of His Life and Times* (London: Charles Baldwyn, 1822)

Anon. (ed.), *An Account of the Siege of Chester* (Chester: P. Broster, 1790)

Anon. (ed.), *Historical Notices of Events Occurring Chiefly in the Reign of Charles I (Nehemiah Wallington)*, Vols 1 and 2 (London: Richard Bentley, 1869)

Anon., *The life of Cornelius Van Tromp, Lieutenant-Admiral of Holland and Westfriesland* (London: J. Orme, 1697)

Anon., *An Humble Representation of the Sad Condition of Many of the Kings Party* (London, 1661)

Anon., *A True Report of the Great Costs and Charges of the Five Hospitals in the City of London* (London, 1650)

Anon., *The Cry of Blood: or, the Horrid Sin of Murther Display'd* (London, 1692)

Anon. (ed.), *A Brief Historical Relation of State Affairs from September 1678 to April 1714 (Narcissus Luttrell)*, Vols 3 and 4 (Oxford: Oxford University Press, 1847)

Anon. (ed.), *Murder and Petty-Treason: or, Bloody News from Southwark* (London, 1677)

Anon., *The lawes against witches...Also, the confession of Mother Lakeland, who was arraigned and condemned for a witch, at Ipswich in Suffolke* (London, 1645)

Anon., *The last words of Coll. Richard Rumbold, Mad. Alicia Lisle, Alderman Henry Cornish, and Mr.Richard Nelthrop who were executed in England and Scotland for high treason in the year 1685* (London, 1685)

Anon., *England's Black Tribunal Containing: I. The Complete Tryal of King Charles the First (...)* (London: R. Freeman, 1747)

Anon. (ed.), *Extracts from a Lancashire Diary, 1663–1678 (Roger Lowe)* (Manchester: T. Sowler & Co., 1876)

Anon., *The Pourtraiture of His royal Highness, Oliver late Lord Protector &c. in his life and death* (London, 1659)

Anon. (ed.), *Memoirs of the Two Last Years of the Reign of King Charles I, by Sir Thomas Herbert* (London: W. Bulmer and Co., 1813)

Anon., *A True Relation of the late King's Death* (London, 1685)

Anon., "The Grand State Funeral of Arthur Duke of Wellington," *The Illustrated London News*, 27 Nov 1852

Anon., *The Cholera Gazette, Consisting of Documents Communicated by the Central Board of Health* (London: S. Highley, 1832)

Various (eds), *Transactions of the Royal Historical Society*, New Series, Vol. 6 (London: Longmans, Green, and Co., 1892) (Consult for the diary of Frederic Gerschow)

Various (eds), *Archaeologia Cantiana*, Vol. 51 (Ashford: Invicta Press, 1939) (Consult for the diary of Isabella Twysden)

Various (eds), *Sussex Archaeological Collections*, Vol. 1, Second Edition (London: John Russell Smith, 1853) (Consult for the diary of Giles Moore)

Various (eds), *Transactions of the Essex Archaeological Society,* Vol. 1 (Colchester: The Essex and West Suffolk Gazette Office, 1858) (Consult for the diary of John Bufton)

Various (eds), *Camden Miscellany*, Vol. 12, Camden Third Series, Vol. 18 (London: Offices of the Society, 1910) (Consult for the diary of Adam Wheeler)

~

Bates, Stephen, "Quiet farewell for Princess Margaret," *The Guardian*, 16 Feb, 2002

Blencowe, R.W. (ed.), *Sydney Papers* (London: John Murray, 1825)

Boas, Samuel (ed.), *The Diary of Thomas Crosfield* (Oxford: Oxford University Press, 1935)

Bray, William (ed.), *The Diary of John Evelyn*, Vols 1 and 2 (London: J.M. Dent & Sons Ltd, 1907)

Carter, Matthew, *A most true and exact relation of that as honourable as unfortunate expedition of Kent, Essex, and Colchester by M.C., a loyall actor in that engagement, Anno Dom. 1648* (London, 1650)

Cartwright, James J. (ed.), *The Memoirs of Sir John Reresby, 1634–1689* (London: Longmans, Green, and Co., 1875)

Clark, Andrew (ed.), *The Life and Times of Anthony Wood*, Vol. 1, Oxford Historical Society, Vol. 19 (Oxford: Clarendon Press, 1891)

Clark, Andrew (ed.), *The Life and Times of Anthony Wood*, Vol. 2, Oxford Historical Society, Vol. 21 (Oxford: Clarendon Press, 1892)

Clark, Andrew (ed.), *The Life and Times of Anthony Wood*, Vol. 3, Oxford Historical Society, Vol. 26 (Oxford: Clarendon Press, 1894)

Clifford, Arthur (ed.), *Tixall Letters; or the Correspondence of the Aston Family*, Vol. 1 (London: Longman, Hurst, Rees, Orme, and Brown, 1815)

Cust, Elizabeth (ed.), *Records of the Cust Family, Series II: The Brownlows of Belton, 1550–1779* (London: Mitchell Hughes and Clarke, 1909)

Defoe, Daniel, *Curious and diverting journies, thro' the whole island of Great-Britain* (London: G. Parker, 1734)

Devereux, Walter Bourchier (ed.), *Lives and Letters of the Devereux, Earls of Essex, 1540–1646*, Vol. 2 (London: John Murray, 1853)

Dunton, John, *A Mourning-Ring in memory of your departed Friend* (London, 1692)

Ellis, Henry (ed.), *Original Letters Illustrative of English History*, Second Series, Vol. 4 (London: Harding and Lepard, 1827)

Ellison Gibson, Thomas, (ed.), *Crosby Records: A Chapter of Lancashire Recusancy*, The Chetham Society, Vol. 12 (Manchester: Charles E. Simms, 1887)

Everett Green, Mary Anne (ed.), *Diary of John Rous* (London: The Camden Society, 1856)

Fairfax, Thomas, *Original Memoirs* (Hargrove and Sons: 1810)

Firth, C.H. (ed.), *The Life of William Cavendish, Duke of Newcastle* (New York: Scribner & Welford, 1886)

Firth, C.H. (ed.), *The Memoirs of Edmund Ludlow* (Oxford: Clarendon Press, 1894)

Foster, J.E. (ed.), *The Diary of Samuel Newton* (Cambridge: Cambridge Antiquarian Society, 1890)

Gill, Harry and Everard L. Guilford (eds), *The Rector's Book (William Sampson)* (Nottingham: H.B. Saxton, 1910)

Green, Robert, *Undertaker and coffin dealer trade card* (London, 1752)

Gregory, Francis, *A thanksgiving sermon for peace abroad* (London: Richard Sare, 1697)

Griffiths, Emily W. (ed.), *Through England On a Side Saddle...Being the Diary of Celia Fiennes* (London: The Leadenhall Press, 1888)

Guizot, Francois P.G. (ed.), *Memoirs of the Life of Colonel Hutchinson (by Lucy Hutchinson)* (London: J.M. Dent & Sons Limited, 1936)

Gunther, R.T. (ed.), *The Diary and Will of Elias Ashmole* (London: Butler & Tanner Ltd, 1927)

H.W., *The House of Mourning* (London, 1640)

Hamilton, William Douglas (ed.), *Calendar of State Papers, Domestic Series, of the Reign of Charles I, 1644–1645* (London: Eyre and Spottiswoode, 1890)

Harvey, Charles, *A Collection of Several Passages Concerning His Late Highnesse Oliver Cromwell, In the Time of His Sickness...Written by One That was Then Groom of His Bed-Chamber* (London, 1659)

Heath, James, *Flagellum: or the Life and Death, Birth and Burial of O. Cromwell* (London, 1665)

Heywood, Thomas (ed.), *The Diary of the Rev. Henry Newcome*, The Chetham Society, Vol. 18 (Manchester: The Chetham Society, 1849)

Hockliffe, E. (ed.), *The Diary of the Rev. Ralph Josselin*, Camden Third Series, Vol. 15 (London: Royal Historical Society, 1908)

Hodgson, J.C. (ed.), *Six North Country Diaries*, Surtrees Society, Vol. 118 (Durham: Andrews and Co., 1910)

Horsfall Turner, J. (ed.), *The Rev. Oliver Heywood: His Autobiography, Diaries, Anecdote and Event Books*, Vol. 1 (Brighouse: 1882)

Horsfall Turner, J. (ed.), *The Rev. Oliver Heywood: His Autobiography, Diaries, Anecdote and Event Books*, Vol. 2 (Brighouse: 1882)

Horsfall Turner, J. (ed.), *The Rev. Oliver Heywood: His Autobiography, Diaries, Anecdote and Event Books*, Vol. 3 (Brighouse: 1883)

Horsfall Turner, J. (ed.), *The Rev. Oliver Heywood: His Autobiography, Diaries, Anecdote and Event Books*, Vol. 4 (Brighouse: 1885)

Hunter, Joseph (ed.), *The Diary of Ralph Thoresby, 1677–1724*, Vol. 1 (London: Henry Colburn and Richard Bentley, 1830)

Jackson, Charles (ed.), *The Autobiography of Mrs Alice Thornton*, Surtrees Society, Vol. 62 (Durham: Andrews and Co., 1875)

Ken, Thomas, *A sermon preached at the funeral of the Right Honourable the Lady Margaret Mainard, at Little Easton in Essex, on the 30th of June, 1682* (London, 1688)

Lee, Matthew Henry (ed.), *Diaries and Letters of Philip Henry* (London: Kegan Paul, Trench & Co., 1882)

Maunde Thompson, Edward (ed.), *Correspondence of the Family of Hatton*, Vols 1 and 2 (London: The Camden Society, 1878)

McClure, Norman Egbert (ed.), *The Letters of John Chamberlain*, Vols 1 and 2 (Philadelphia: The American Philosophical Society, 1939)

Misson, M., *Memoirs and Observations in His Travels Over England* (London, 1719)

Morehouse, Henry James (ed.), *Extracts from the Diary of the Rev. Robert Meeke* (London: H.G. Bohn, 1874)

Morley, Henry (ed.), *A Journal of the Plague Year in 1665...By Daniel Defoe* (London: George Routledge & Sons, Limited, 1896)

Noon Talfourd, Thomas (ed.), *The Works of Charles Lamb* (London: Edward Moxon, 1848)

Orchard Halliwell, James (ed.), *The Autobiography and Correspondence of Sir Simonds d'Ewes*, Vols 1 and 2 (London: Richard Bentley, 1845)

Palmes, William (ed.), *The Life of Mrs Dorothy Lawson, of St Antony's, near Newcastle-on-Tyne* (London: Charles Dolman, 1855)

Raines, F.R. (ed.), *The Journal of Nicholas Assheton*, The Chetham Society, Vol. 14 (Manchester: The Chetham Society, 1848)

Ralph, Philip Lee, *Sir Humphrey Mildmay: Royalist Gentleman: Glimpses of the English Scene, 1633–1652* (New Brunswick: Rutgers University Press, 1947)

Roberts, George (ed.), *Diary of Walter Yonge* (London: The Camden Society, 1848)

Romillys (eds), *The Life of Sir Samuel Romilly*, Vol. 2 (London: John Murray, 1842)

Scott, Walter (ed.), *A Collection of Scarce and Valuable Tracts*, Vol. 1 (London: anonymous printer, 1809)

Scott, Walter (ed.), *Original Memoirs Written During the Great Civil War: Being the Life of Sir Henry Slingsby, and Memoirs of Captain Hodgson* (Edinburgh: James Ballantyne & Co., 1806)

Severn, Charles (ed.), *Diary of the Rev. John Ward* (London: Henry Colburn, 1839)

Sheppard, William, *The Offices of Constables, Church-Wardens, Overseers of the Poor, Supravisors of the High-wayes, Treasurers of the County-Stock, and Some Other Lesser Country Officers* (London, 1650)

Storey, Matthew (ed.), *Two East Anglian Diaries, 1641–1729: Isaac Archer and William Coe*, Suffolk Records Society, Vol. 36 (Woodbridge: The Boydell Press, 1994)

Taylor Lewis, Thomas (ed.), *Letters of the Lady Brilliana Harley* (London: Camden Society, 1854)

Timings, E.K. (ed.), *Calendar of State Papers, Domestic Series, James II, Volume I, February–December 1685* (London: Her Majesty's Stationery Office, 1960)

Verney, Margaret M. (ed.), *Memoirs of the Verney Family*, Vols 1 and 2 (London: Longmans, Green, and Co., 1904)

Walker, Anthony (ed.), *Memoir of Lady Warwick: Also Her Diary* (London: The Religious Tract Society, 1847)

Warburton, William (ed.), *The History of the Rebellion and Civil Wars in England (Clarendon)*, Vol. 7 (Oxford: Clarendon Press, 1826)

Washbourn, John (ed.), *Bibliotheca Gloucestrensis: A Collection of Scarce and Curious Tracts, Relating to the County and City of Gloucester* (Gloucester: 1825)

Wheatley, Henry B. (ed.), *The Diary of Samuel Pepys*, Vols 1 and 2 (New York: Random House, pref. 1893)

Whittie, John, *An Exact Diary of the Late Expedition of His Illustrious Highness the Prince of Orange* (London, 1689)

Williams, J.B., *Memoirs of the Life, Character, and Writings of the Rev. Matthew Henry* (London: J. Holdsworth, 1828)

Williamson, George C. (ed.), *Lady Anne Clifford, Countess of Dorset, Pembroke & Montgomery, 1590–1676: Her Life, Letters, and Work* (Kendal: Titus Wilson and Son, 1922)

Wilton Rix, S. (ed.), *The Diary and Autobiography of Edmund Bohun Esq.* (Beccles: Read Crisp, 1853)

Winthrop, Robert C. (ed.), *Life and Letters of John Winthrop*, Vol. 1 (Boston: Little, Brown, and Company, 1869)

Worthington Barlow, T., *Cheshire: Its Historical and Literary Associations (With A Reprint of the Diary of Edward Burghall)* (Manchester: John Gray Bell, 1855)

Yearwood, Randolph, *The Penitent Murderer. Being An Exact Narrative Of the Life and Death of Nathaniel Butler* (London: T. Newcomb, 1659)

For a comprehensive list of seventeenth-century diaries it is strongly recommended by the author that readers consult the following work:

Matthews, William, *British Diaries: An Annotated Bibliography of British Diaries Written between 1442 and 1942* (Berkeley: University of California Press, 1950)

Selected Secondary Literature

Appleby, David J. and Andrew Hopper (eds), *Battle-scarred: Mortality, medical care, and military welfare in the British Civil Wars* (Manchester: Manchester University Press, 2018)

Beattie, J.M., *Crime and the Courts in England, 1660–1800* (Princeton: Princeton University Press, 1986)

Bentley, David, *English Criminal Justice in the Nineteenth Century* (London: The Hambledon Press, 1998)

Bland, Olivia, *The Royal Way of Death* (London: Constable and Company Ltd, 1986)

Blatchly, John, "The lost and mutilated memorials of the Bovile and Wingfield families at Letheringham," in *Proceedings of the Suffolk Institute for Archaeology and History* 33, No. 2 (1974): 168–194

Carlton, Charles, *Going to the Wars: The Experience of the British Civil Wars, 1638–1651* (London: Routledge, 1992)

Cowen Orlin, Lena, "Empty Vessels," in *Everyday Objects: Medieval and Early Modern Material Culture and Its Meanings*, edited by Tara Hamling and Catherine Richardson, 299–307 (Farnham: Ashgate Publishing Limited, 2012)

Cressy, David, *Birth, Marriage, and Death: Ritual, Religion, and the Life-cycle in Tudor and Stuart England* (Oxford: Oxford University Press, 1997)

Davidson, Ian, *Voltaire: A Life* (New York: Pegasus Books, 2012)

Dolan, Francis E., *Dangerous Familiars: Representations of Domestic Crime in England, 1550–1700* (New York: Cornell University Press, 2016)

Donagan, Barbara, *War in England, 1642-1649* (Oxford: Oxford University Press, 2008)

Farrer, Edward, *A List of Monumental Brasses Remaining in the County of Suffolk* (Norwich: Agas H. Goose, 1903)

Gaskill, Malcolm, *Crime and Mentalities in Early Modern England* (Cambridge: Cambridge University Press, 2000)

Gittings, Clare, *Death, Burial, and the Individual in Early Modern England* (London: Routledge, 1988)

Gittings, Clare, "Sacred and secular: 1558–1660," in *Death in England: An Illustrated History*, edited by Peter C. Jupp and Clare Gittings, 147–173 (Manchester: Manchester University Press, 1999)

Goose, Nigel and Nesta Evans, "Wills as an Historical Source," in *When Death Do Us Part: Understanding and Interpreting the Probate Records of Early Modern England*, edited by Tom Arkell, Nesta Evans and Nigel Goose, 38–71 (Oxford: Leopard's Head Press Limited, 2004)

Gruber Von Arni, Eric, "Who Cared? Military Nursing During the English Civil Wars and Interregnum, 1642-60," in *British Military and Naval Medicine, 1600-1830*, edited by Geoffrey L. Hudson, 121–144 (Boston: Rodopi, 2007)

Harding, Vanessa, "Burial of the plague dead in early modern London," in *Epidemic Disease in London*, edited by J.A.I. Champion (London: Centre for Metropolitan History, 1993)

Harding, Vanessa, *The Dead and the Living in Paris and London, 1500–1670* (Cambridge: Cambridge University Press, 2002)

Hindle, Steve, *On the Parish? The Micro-Politics of Poor Relief in Rural England, c.1550–1750* (Oxford: Clarendon Press, 2004)

Houlbrooke, Ralph, *Death, Religion, and the Family in England, 1480-1750* (Oxford: Clarendon Press, 1998)

Hunt, Tristram, *The English Civil War at First Hand* (London: Penguin Books, 2011)

Jalland, Pat, *Death in the Victorian Family* (Oxford: Oxford University Press, 1999)

Laurence, Anne, *Parliamentary Army Chaplains, 1642-1651* (Woodbridge: Boydell & Brewer Ltd., 1990)

Llewellyn, Nigel, *The Art of Death: Visual Culture in the English Death Ritual, c.1500–c.1800* (London: Reaktion Books Ltd, 1997)

MacMillan, Ken (ed.), *Stories of True Crime in Tudor and Stuart England* (Abingdon: Routledge, 2015)

Marshall, Peter, *Beliefs and the Dead in Reformation England* (Oxford: Oxford University Press, 2002)

Martin, Randall, *Women, Murder, and Equity in Early Modern England* (Abingdon: Routledge, 2008)

McCray Beier, Lucinda, *Sufferers and Healers: The Experience of Illness in Seventeenth-century England* (London: Routledge & Kegan Paul, 1987)

McMahon, Vanessa, *Murder in Shakespeare's England* (London: Hambledon and London, 2004)

Parsons, Catherine E., *All Saints' Church Horseheath* (Cambridge: Cambridge University Press, 1911)

Phillippy, Patricia, *Women, Death, and Literature in Post-Reformation England* (Cambridge: Cambridge University Press, 2002)

Pincus, Steve, *1688: The First Modern Revolution* (London: Yale University Press, 2009)

Pollock, Linda A., *With Faith and Physic: The Life of a Tudor Gentlewoman, Lady Grace Mildmay, 1552–1620* (London: Collins & Brown, 1993)

Roberts, G., *The History of Lyme-Regis, Dorset, From the Earliest Periods to the Present Day* (Sherborne: Langdon and Harker, 1823)

Roberts, George, *The Life, Progresses, and Rebellion of James, Duke of Monmouth*, Vol. 2 (London: Longman, Brown, Green, and Longmans, 1844)

Schen, Claire, *Charity and Lay Piety in Reformation London, 1500–1620* (Aldershot: Ashgate Publishing Limited, 2002)

Sharpe, James, *Crime in Early Modern England, 1550–1750* (Abingdon: Routledge, 2013)

Sharpe, James, *A Fiery & Furious People: A History of Violence in England* (London: Random House Books, 2016)

Sherlock, Peter, *Monuments and Memory in Early Modern England* (Aldershot: Ashgate Publishing Limited, 2008)

Slack, Paul, *The Impact of Plague in Tudor and Stuart England* (London: Routledge & Kegan Paul, 1985)

Spencer, Charles, *Killers of the King: The Men Who Dared to Execute Charles I* (London: A&C Black, 2014)

Walker, Garthine, *Crime, Gender, and Social Order in Early Modern England* (Cambridge: Cambridge University Press, 2003)

Wrightson, Keith, *Ralph Tailor's Summer: A Scrivener, His City, and the Plague* (New Haven: Yale University Press, 2011)

Wrigley, E.A., R.S. Davies, J.E. Oeppen and R.S. Schofield, *English population history from family reconstitution, 1580–1837* (Cambridge: Cambridge University Press, 1997)

Wroughton, John, *A Community at War: The Civil War in Bath and North Somerset, 1642-1650* (Bath: The Lansdown Press, 1992)

Index